Bending Time

ALSO BY PATRICK PAUL GARLINGER

When Thought Turns to Light

Seeds of Light

Bending Time

The Power to Live in the Now

PATRICK PAUL GARLINGER

Anastasis Books
New York, NY

Bending Time: The Power to Live in the Now

This book is to be regarded as a reference source and is not intended to replace professional medical advice or prescribe the use of any technique as a form of treatment for physical, emotional, or medical problems without the advice of your physician or therapist. The author and the publisher disclaim any liability arising directly or indirectly from the use of this book.

Paperback ISBN: 978-0-9985563-2-1
E-book ISBN: 978-0-9985563-3-8
Library of Congress Control Number: 2018936001

Distributed by Epigraph Publishing Service

Cover and book design by Nuno Moreira, NM Design

Anastasis Books
New York, NY
www.anastasisbooks.com

Contents

Preface

This book, like my previous volume of channeled writing, *Seeds of Light*, was written over the course of about two months. The book's transmission began in May 2016, while I was traveling abroad for work and still preparing *Seeds of Light* for publication. I had not expected the next volume to come so quickly after I finished the first one, nor under those particular circumstances. The book began one evening with this channeled transmission, directed at me personally:

> *You worked and spent time abroad in an old city you once knew. That was an experience of two points of time coming together, which you had not expected—the time of your memory and the time of your present moment. And you realized that those two points of time could appear to collapse and connect all at once.*
>
> *You all experience this as you walk through life, through the places that you have seen and been, and the places that you are now experiencing. But the important point at that time was the relationship between your memory of the place, the city of Madrid, and your experience of it in the present moment; you saw both the city as it was at the time, and your memory of it as it was before.*
>
> *Now, this is a very common practice—you all do this every day—and yet you do not realize or appreciate experiencing the same place again and again. Except when you discover how jarring and profound it is to see a place you knew when you were someone else, through the eyes of the person you are now. This time, you saw Madrid completely differently, in ways you could not have done when you experienced Madrid in the past. When you saw a building, you saw it through new eyes and old eyes at the same time.*
>
> *This is a unique way to see what is happening in the world, but the changes are usually so minor that you do not*

notice the miracle that surrounds you. For you are never the same when you experience what you think of as the same time and place. No, you are entirely different. The previous moment has altered you irrevocably and completely, in ways that you cannot appreciate. Each second marks a unique universe of its own, and the next a creation of a world entirely different from the one you knew before. Yet you maintain coherence between these two points of time. You experience time and space as linear and consistent. But every moment is actually a new creation, at each point.

Experiencing a memory of Madrid from a previous consciousness, and the Madrid of today… Yes, much of it looked the same. You saw the buildings that were there ten years ago. And yet you perceived at each moment the discrepancy between your current reality and that of your memory, and that had a jarring effect on your being. You inhabited both experiences, both moments, at the same time.

This occurs for many of you when you return to a place you have not been in a long time. The effect is the same: two consciousnesses coming together at one point in time, the memory of the past surviving as the vestige of that prior consciousness. So it is not just the memory in the sense of having a snapshot or visual, but the connection between two types of experience, two consciousnesses, as one experiences the same place with another consciousness.

We will explore in this book the role of memory in the creation of consciousness, and how that works with time and space, and in particular, the creation of a new consciousness. We will teach you how to bend time and space, and to understand what it means to be in time and space as manifestations of Light in a deeper way than we have previously explored. We will help you to see the ways in which your most mundane experiences are actually miracles, and teach you precisely how you are truly manifesting in each moment, in each second, in ways that defy your current understanding.

And so we began writing *Bending Time.*

As was the case with *Seeds of Light*, I downloaded each transmission, and sometimes several, in a single day. At times the Council of Light—the collective of Light Beings who transmit their messages to me—wanted me to write faster, but occasionally I found myself resisting their call. That resistance was a result of my own ego's questions about what this endeavor might mean. Was I now to serve as the spokesperson for the Council of Light, as they have called themselves (a name I admittedly have struggled to embrace)? Was I to give up other plans? How should I organize my life around this work?

I am still pursuing the answers to these questions.

In the course of receiving their teachings, I also unexpectedly found myself resisting some of the material, particularly around their treatment of mothers and fathers. Since I am not a mouthpiece, but a conversant engaged in a dialogue, I found myself pressing for additional clarification or simply asserting that particular messages challenged either spiritual wisdom I had received from others, or my personal understanding of the nature of reality. (The reader will find my questions in the text offset in italics.)

Still, as much as I might question some of their teachings, it is not my place to censor or edit them to conform to my own views. Instead, I have endeavored to make them as clear and accessible as possible, while still respecting their unique voice, so different from my own.

Like its predecessor, *Bending Time* does not take a perfectly linear path. Each section is like a piece of a puzzle, and together these pieces reveal a coherent picture. To assist the reader in putting the puzzle together, I have included an introduction that provides an overview of the material from *Seeds of Light* and outlines how certain concepts are further developed in this work. It is my hope that, for those who are not familiar with the first volume, this overview will make *Bending Time* more accessible. At a minimum, the introduction will provide all readers with a basic roadmap of this book's journey through higher consciousness.

Longer than the first installment, this work raises questions that I had not previously contemplated about how to live fully in the present moment, and in doing so, transform how we relate to each other and to the world itself. *Bending Time* builds on the insights first articulated in *Seeds of Light* about how our egos are structured in relation to time and space. In doing so, it develops an entirely novel way of thinking about how we approach our relationships with other human beings and the physical world, through the concept of *bending* time and space. Our conventional approach to change is quite often to push the world to conform with our own vision of what life should be, using words to manipulate or brute force to coerce others into acceding to our will. *Bending Time* charts another path—one that I am still learning to incorporate in my own life, but which allows us to experience the present moment as it truly is, unburdened by the emotional pain of the past. Rather than trying to "change" the world around us by imposing our views of what should be, we can change ourselves—and thereby open ourselves to a new experience of the world. It is my hope that this work will raise your consciousness and help you to live, fully and powerfully, in the present moment.

Patrick Paul Garlinger
New York, New York
October 2016–November 2017

Introduction

My first volume of channeled writing, *Seeds of Light*, addressed the nature of the human mind. Specifically, it undertook the task of explaining how our consciousness is based on separation—that is, how we view each other as separate beings, distinguished from each other in time and space. This is how we form a sense of self: We believe that we are separate from all other objects in space and time, and so we are engaged in a constant effort to differentiate ourselves. Our consciousness looks at the world in this way: *I am me and not you, and now and in the next second, I am still me and you are still you, and I am still not you, and vice-versa.*

And although we believe that our existence is one of separation, science tells us that our eyes deceive us. The physical world is much more complex than what our vision can capture, and quantum physics has altered our understanding of topics such as matter, time, and gravity. Following that line of thinking, and rejecting separation as the truth of human consciousness, *Seeds of Light* advanced a radical new conception of who we are as human beings.

A brief overview of its basic tenets will be helpful in understanding the new material presented in *Bending Time.* As mentioned above, separation is the starting point for our typical human consciousness. But our minds do not stop with separation or differentiation. Instead, they move almost seamlessly into judgments and evaluations. Our minds identify everything as separate from us, in time and space—and what's more, those differences almost always take the form of value judgments. Not only are you *not* me, but you are either *better* or *worse* than me.

And at their core, our evaluations are a reflection of our existential fear of death. To start with, separation means that other people and objects can cease to exist, while I continue to exist separately from them. But the corollary is that I, too, can cease to exist … and the rest of the world will continue to exist without *me.* To paraphrase Descartes, I am separate, therefore I am. But because I am separate, I can die.

Our minds' movement from separation to judgment and the underlying fear of non-existence means that our minds tend to evaluate the exterior world for whether it supports or threatens the self. One of the ways that our minds make this calculation easier is to work in simple binaries—good and bad, better or worse, dark and light. The categories that we use to distinguish ourselves also almost always take binary form: man or woman, gay or straight, majority or minority. Binary categorization extends to nearly every aspect of our lives. And this is the trap of the human mind, which requires a self that is differentiated from others based on categories.

Our language—the words we use to describe ourselves—reinforces our belief in our binary separation. The Light Beings talk about this as *constitution*: how we constitute ourselves, or co-create ourselves, with the words that we use to describe ourselves. In other words, description is not actually description; it is creation. We are literally forming who we are based on our perceptions of separation and our assignment of categories, which are filled with judgments and evaluations, to each and every other human being. This is the crux of the "collective consciousness." It is the sum of the world as we experience it. It is not reality, but it is our creation of it and, as such, is how reality appears to us.

Seeds of Light was focused on demonstrating how this construct of the mind plays out in numerous facets of life, and in pulling back the veil, so to speak, the book sought to reveal that our minds do not have to operate in that manner. Instead, we can access a different type of consciousness: what the Light Beings call the Christ Consciousness. That is a phrase that might rankle some readers, and in many ways, it is supposed to. The figure of Jesus holds enormous power in our collective consciousness—either in the form embraced by various strands of Christianity, or in the rejection of that form by many who regard Jesus as a tool of oppression wielded by the very strands of Christianity that purport to worship him. For many, he is a symbol of the Divine, and for others, a symbol of religious intolerance and moral dogma. Either way, the Christ occupies an enormous symbolic space in our collective consciousness.

Seeds of Light offered a radical reinterpretation of the Christ—one that might make him less a historical figure and more a model that we each can embody. In this way, he becomes a figure like the Buddha. Rather than treat the Christ as a figure of worship, the Light Beings exhort us to see the Christ as a state of consciousness—one that we all have the potential to access, although very few do the necessary work to do so. The book reinterpreted the crucifixion and the resurrection in more metaphorical terms—the crucifixion is the attachment to the ego and its linear view of time, and the resurrection is our inherent power to give birth to ourselves again and again, from one moment to the next.

The Christ Consciousness thus embraces the view that we recreate ourselves in each moment. There is no past and there is no future. Those are all mental formulations, or constructions. There is only the present moment. Yet our egos too often lead us to replicate the past within the present moment—so that we can anticipate and control the future. The Christ Consciousness calls for us to relinquish our attachments to our identity and our adherence to the past as the template for the future. It is truly the embodiment of the "now," of the present moment. By relinquishing our traditional perceptions of time, and in particular, our attachment to the past as a way to create the future, we can access the Christ Consciousness.

In this way, *Seeds of Light* asks us to let go of our limiting beliefs and recognize that we are not separate from God or the Divine. We are each a spark of the Creator, what the Light Beings call a "Seed of Light." In other words, each of us is made up of the same living energy that makes up all life, including the stars and planets. Our powers to create our experiences in life are far more vast than we realize. Yet we use them all the time, now, to create a world built on separation, where everything is evaluated as a possible threat. Instead of creating something new in each moment, we carry the past with us, from early traumas to our parents' own baggage, into the future—and continue to confine ourselves to what came before.

Against that background, *Seeds of Light* reframed a number of basic tenets, such as blasphemy, compassion, and forgiveness. Blasphemy, for example, was redefined not as speaking ill of God, but as the failure to recognize the divinity of every person. Compassion is not the feeling we associate with caring for the needs of others, but rather the recognition that all is in divine right order, and that every person is a spark of the Creator who is utterly perfect in their imperfections. Forgiveness does not simply release someone from wrongdoing, but actually rewrites the past, so that the present no longer carries with it the energy of some past grievance. Our ability to forgive is one of our greatest powers, and the training of the mind to release the past through forgiving regularly is a portal to the Christ Consciousness.

Bending Time develops these concepts further by deepening our understanding of how we relate to time and space, which, in turn, deepens our understanding of our powers of creation. It does this by focusing on how we *relate* to each other, and to the world, through time and space, with special emphasis on time. Much of the basic material was already presented in *Seeds of Light*, but the role of time in the formation of our consciousness is developed by an examination of how time informs our relationship to our parents, our bodies, our loved ones, and ultimately, the world itself.

The essential point of this book is that how we relate to time is the matrix through which all of our human connections are made and formed. Just as we relate to time, we relate to the world as a whole, including all of the people in it. Much of that is tied to the role of memory and perception as we evaluate what appears before us. We see with old eyes, with the eyes of the past, instead of seeing anew. Most people would say that this is the only way we can relate to each other with any meaning, and that such memory is necessary to avoid repeating the pitfalls of history. *Bending Time* says that this is not true, however, and that it is our relationship to time, and how our consciousness is currently formed *around* certain concepts of time, that is the pitfall.

Much of the book elaborates on a corollary of this principle—that we view the present through the eyes of the past. We relate to others in ways that replicate the past and attempt to avoid the unknown, and in that sense, we never allow ourselves to appreciate or honor the full expression of another human being's existence. Our way of making sense of things—by relying on what we already know—limits us to a small sampling of our infinite possibilities as human beings. Much of our sense of self is premised on the idea that we need certain categories of identity to be seen, to be heard, and therefore to be loved—because those categories are what we know, and have learned. But that concept comes at the cost of the infinite possibilities with which we might otherwise have expressed our being, in new and varied ways.

Similarly, we rarely relate to the present moment as it is—complete, whole, and full of love. We relate to it through our sense of lack, and we compare it to what was and what we think it should be. We examine the world through our memories of what came before, so we are constantly evaluating what is now against what was, and in doing so, we never actually experience the present moment as it is. We only see it through the lens of the past. So we continue to re-create the present moment, often through our memories, in the same way. The world as we experience it is not reality; we are creating a version of reality that we experience in each moment, based on our perceptions from the past.

As the title conveys, the book's central focus is the concept of "bending time." In some ways, it is another way of referring to creation or manifestation. But the idea of bending time is tied to the idea of *how* we experience time and space. And by experiencing it differently, we can actually learn to *bend* time and space—that is, we can align with a different reality than the one we are experiencing in this moment. Instead of co-creating the past or trying to will a future through force, coercion, persuasion, and the usual means of influencing others, we can *bend* ourselves into that experience. It is a way of aligning ourselves to possibilities, rather than forcing them into being.

This is true of people and experiences. Rather than trying to change your relationships by making the other person into what you think they should be, you can align yourself with their higher self, allowing your own presence to encourage them to access their own true nature and to shape their lives in a new and powerful way. Imagine being with people who suddenly act from their highest good, opening up their hearts, being vulnerable, and accessing new levels of creativity and compassion.

The idea of "bending time" is about relating to what you experience differently so that the fullest expression of what is possible comes into alignment with your experience of reality. You see and experience a different world because you are aligned with a different possibility—one that is not based on replicating the past or trying to shape reality through force. Instead, it comes from understanding that you are Light, you are a spark of the Creator, with infinite capabilities of creating, which are no longer limited based on old assumptions about what the world looks like.

Bending Time asks us to regard our connection with our fellow human beings as a collective endeavor of allowing each person to express their essence as fully and authentically as possible, without requiring them to be what *we* expect them to be. It is an invitation to a world of fullness—that is the word the Light Beings use to describe the truth of the present moment and the truth of who we are. Human beings are "full" in that we are already complete; there is nothing outside of us that is needed to make us feel whole. The Christ Consciousness knows that the belief that we are flawed, unworthy, and unlovable is simply the byproduct of the mind's separation from all that is.

The book offers not only valuable insights into human consciousness and relationships, but some very practical advice along the way, as well. Some of that advice involves working directly with your perception of time. Some of it involves verbal formulations—phrases that are themselves claims or statements about who and what we are as humans. One of the formulations is "I am the Christ in form reborn." If the word "Christ" raises too much resistance, you can say, "I am the Light in form reborn." Either one is a statement that claims your true nature. You are, of course, the Light—this was the teaching of *Seeds of Light*. You are also the Christ, and that statement claims the truth of your relationship to time and space. So if you can overcome your resistance to the word "Christ," the phrase is an especially potent means of accessing the higher self, which knows that there is no time or space, except for the present moment as you are creating it. Another powerful claim to truth is "I am here with you just as you are." It is a statement of alignment with the other person in the present moment, and one that relinquishes your expectations of how they should be.

If the concepts in *Bending Time* are embraced, humanity can wake up to a reality more profound and beautiful than we could have imagined. So many people are waking up to their true selves. Now is the time—and that phrase has a dual meaning. Now is the time because there is only the now. But it is also a call to action in the form of waking up and living your life differently. The present, as we have constructed it, is a world where life is quickly becoming unsustainable. So let us co-create a new realm, where our fullness and our interconnectedness are the guiding principles for how we relate to our selves, to each other, and to the world as a whole.

Part I: Creation

1. Memory as Creation

You all use memory for the creation of a world—a world that you experienced at a particular moment in time and space, and have since begun to experience in different ways. Yes, memory is a powerful form of creation—one of your most basic forms, which you use to manipulate time and space. You do not think of it as manipulating time and space, and that is one of the points we make, for you must understand the role of memory in the creation of your present world.

With memory, you bring two different worlds, in time and space, together at the same moment of consciousness. No, you do not experience them in the same way; you experience one as memory and the other as the present. But this is not a distinction that is important right now. Suffice it to say that you have the ability to recreate the world—a partial recreation—through your memory. Your experience of that moment in time and space may be altered, and it may not correspond to the past as you really experienced it. But that is not important. Our point is that, at a given moment, when you experience memory, you are creating through your intellectual faculties a world that did not exist in time and space the moment before. You are joining two worlds. You are joining the world that exists now, and that you experience in the present moment, with the world based on your memory of that place.

Why is this important?[1]

It is important because we are beginning to delve into the mastery of thought and mind and creative thinking. As to that, you must understand your creative faculties—your powers to create, in this realm—and that you often create through the power of your memory. You are constantly recreating worlds, and doing

---

1 As a reminder to the reader, questions formatted in italics on a separate line from the rest of the text are those that I have posed directly to the Light Beings in response to their transmission.

so by bending time and space through your memories, which are aspects of the world that you once experienced. Is that not amazing? You do not experience it as amazing. You experience it as mundane and boring, and you often feel burdened by your memories. But that is the point: You do not see this as a marvelous faculty of creation. You do not see it as a part of your powers as Seeds of Light who are creating this realm. No, you see it as a burden, a weight, and think to yourself, *Oh, if I could just clear the past and not have these horrible memories that weigh me down so, I might be free, free*. And yes, you *could* be free to recreate in this moment, anew. And you are doing so already with your memories, with the weight of the past.

You do not *need* to create this weight. But you do, and that is why we begin with memory, as a manifestation of your ability to bend time and space.

That memory is your primary tool of creation in this realm is not to suggest that it is your *only* tool. It is simply the one you use most readily for navigating time and space. You have many tools of manifestation—ways of bringing things into form with your mind. And we will examine them more throughout the course of this book. For now, please understand that our focus is on helping you understand the ways that you manifest, though you do not see it as such. You may already see yourself building with your hands or painting or writing or playing music, etc., all of which lead to you using language and materials. But we are first dealing with manifestation at the level of the mind.

Your memory is incredibly powerful, but you do not see it as powerful. You see it as mundane, because you do not see it for what it really is: the potential of your infinite imagination. Yes, you use your ability to create images, first and foremost, but you rely on material from what you have already seen. You recycle images, and in so doing you recycle and revive the vision of yourself from when those images first imprinted themselves on your consciousness. And so you are constantly recycling, not creating anew—just as you do with your identities and ways of being and relating to others. You recycle constantly—in ways that hold you back—because it is familiar, and comfortable, and safe.

But we are talking here about the possibility of re-creating in the realm of the mind through vision, through images, and that does not involve recycling the past, using memory. Memory is your primary means of visual recreation, and you use it all the time to relive the past and bring it into the present. You meet the present through your memory, through the vision of the past, and in so doing consistently bend time and space. This is powerful, yet you don't appreciate that, for you bend time and space to stay connected with the past, rather than creating something new in each moment.

But you can liberate yourself from your memory without having to forget. This is the first step to true freedom from the past.

∞

The existence of your world begins in the mind's eye, as a creative faculty, as a form of bending time and space. You can be in one location in time and space, and at that same time your mind can be elsewhere, traveling, creatively and visually, to another realm or realms, even ones that you have never seen or imagined before, and that have no prior reference in your memory or experience.

Your creation begins in the mind, in the mind's eye, as a visual faculty. Even though many of you work with words, there's actually a part of you—the creative part of you—that is already working in images, working in pictures in your mind's eye. And that part may be drawing from images and pieces of your past to create a new future. In other words, there's always some anchor in the past, some connection to what you know, even if it is wholly new in the sense that we just described. We are not speaking of a new world or dimension so foreign that it defies your brain's capacity to imagine it.

We want to say that creation can always partake of the past, of your knowledge of form, without necessarily being *derived* from the past. This is a key distinction, because most of you create versions of the past in ways that replicate the same stories, and so draw from the same stories and do not create new forms. Those of you who create are most of the time doing so in the same ways again and again, so that you experience the same storylines again and again. So the images you create are often replicas of the past. Not just based on the same form. In other words, you are resurrecting yourselves again and again in the same storyline that you have already experienced, even though your creative powers are more vast, and capable of finding entirely new realms and new stories. But you do not appreciate your own power, and so you do not use it properly.

The power of the Christ Consciousness is the power to create from the past without being derivative of the past. To refashion yourselves in new forms that resemble the past, but do not carry the past with them. To rebirth yourselves as a new person, in a way that otherwise can resemble, in form, your life, but does not carry with it the baggage—emotional baggage, fear, doubt—that you experience. Your life is perfect just as it is in its current form, in all ways, but you do not experience your life that way. Even if your life appears to be good, or looks exactly as you want it to be, you often experience it as not (good) enough. The Christ Consciousness allows for the creation of a new world that partakes of past form—but without the past stories. We will show you how to inhabit this consciousness, and how to lay your fears and doubts to rest.

∞

To understand your creative faculties and how you produce the world you experience, you must first understand how you relate to the process of creation. And you currently relate to creation primarily through the form of energy known as money. Yes, we are talking about money as a creative force, as a form of energy, and that is what it allows you to do: create. You create your lives with money, and like time, it is something that you are obsessed with—even when you have negative views of it. It is a topic that is—again like time—something you consider constantly, asking whether you have enough or should have more or how to make more.

Creative and powerful, money functions as a means of exchange in your world, translating what you do into something that can then be translated into what someone else does. You perform a service or create an object, and that is exchanged with someone else for that money, which in turn allows you to procure something that someone *else* does or makes. In other words, money is the means by which you negotiate separation and the exchange of energy between you and others. In a nonform realm, you would not need money to exchange energy; you would have other means. Here, however, the primary means of exchanging energy with another person in the form of goods and services is through the medium of money. In that way, it is essential to your existence; it is the purest form of energy in this realm, in that it serves as the most basic energy transfer system in your world.

There is nothing wrong with that; it is not the only means, but it is the means you have. Simply acknowledge that money is what allows you to engage with and connect with all other forms of energy in your realm. Of course, there are forms of energy that do not require money. For example, we do not require money in return for *our* transmission, but if this transmission is produced into a book and circulated, then others will exchange its energy for money. That is how your system works.

And we are focusing on money because it is currently essential, like time, to your existence in this realm. And like time, it is something that actually exists and does not exist. Money is what you have agreed upon, collectively, as the means by which energy transfers are negotiated in your world.

There is nothing wrong with that. It means that you must negotiate with and through this form of currency, which was once physical and is now a sort of linguistic agreement—something that is based on words and agreements. You used to go to the bank, where you stored bills or gold or objects that stood for value, but you have since moved to words and records kept in electronic format. So this is an agreement, about the transfer of energy, that allows you to obtain goods and services from others, and is fundamental to your way of life in this world at this time.

There is nothing wrong with that. So why do you reject it, why do you blame it for all of the ills of the world? Money raises strange issues for many people, for money has so many associations in your realm. Many of you reject money. That is, you regard it as a sort of necessary evil, where you must have enough to barter and buy the goods that you need to survive physically. Yet you somehow regard it as beneath you. Understand that money is just a form of energy. And that is why you are misguided in rejecting it outright in the name of spirituality, or embracing some sort of poverty in the name of allegiance with those who are less fortunate. This is a form of martyrdom that does little but spread a poverty consciousness through the realm.

It is true that it is the primary mode of transfer, and so there are ways in which money seems negative, and you label it *dirty* or *filthy*, but this is to conflate the structures that you have put in place with the energy itself. Those structures determine how and when the energy flows from some to others, and this has allowed some to exercise a great deal of control and to amass much more money than others. That is a system that seeks to exploit the condition of separation from which you suffer. But to criticize money as the root of evil is to mistake the structures the collective consciousness have put in place for the actual energy that passes through them.

It is the structure that is the problem, not the energy transfer. Money is a creative force, agreed upon as the mechanism for energy exchange in this physical realm. That is it. Nothing more. And it is fundamental, so you must begin to look at money as the building block for your creation.

Now we can connect your relationship to time with your relationship to money. For while time is an omnipresent aspect of your consciousness as humans, so, too, is money. As the transfer of energy in and through time and space, it is fundamental to how you relate to each other through separation. Time and money are both forms of a collective agreement; you agree with each other regarding time, and you agree with each other regarding the transfer of energy between "separate" beings in this realm.

There is a phrase—"time is money"—that captures your dual commitment to these two concepts, so pervasive is your awareness of time and money. Time and money are nearly the same insofar as time is what allows you to experience a transfer of energy, to experience the expenditure of energy in a living body throughout the course of a life, and money is the means by which you sustain this body over time, so that you can experience time itself. Money is therefore the energy that allows you to experience time, and is fundamental to your experience of time.

∞

Just as you do with money, many of you ask questions like: *How do I save time? How do I make time?* This is something you ask each other, speaking of time as something you lack or something over which you have no control, when you *do*. Yet you act as if you don't. You act as if time were an agreement that happens without you, and as if there were nothing you could do about it. Time passes, and if you just sit there, time will pass without you. You say things like, *I don't have enough time*, or, *Look at how the time flies.*

And yet this is not true. Time is merely an instrument of perception, and you can control it if you learn to. You can change the ways you perceive time. Yes, there is an aspect you cannot control, which is that ultimately your life will shift form and move out of the physical. This is inevitable, because of the need for you to take on other forms. Right now, you are in a finite form, because it allows you to experience the world in a particular way. There are fantasies of immortality, and you have ideas about freezing yourselves or doing other things to extend your life.

It is odd, we say, because you do not really appreciate your life as it is now. Why expand something that you don't fully appreciate? You seem to want to stretch time in the hopes of achieving something that you make no effort to achieve. Instead, learn to work with time as it presently exists, which is all there is—the present moment. You know this, many of you, as a spiritual teaching and something of a platitude, like, "Just stay in the present moment."

What this truly means is that you are creators of your own experience of time, and therefore you have the ability to stretch and bend time, to perceive it differently. You may think that time passes quickly or slowly, but this is your perception of your relationship to what is occurring at the present moment. When time passes quickly, that is not the speed of time. No—it is your *perception* of time. Why does it appear to pass quickly? Because you do not relate to what is occurring with resistance. No, you relate to what is occurring with incredible delight, so much so that you lose track of time. You are no longer focused on something negative—you experience something positive, and so you lose time. Or more accurately, you lose your perception of time. When you are bored or anxious, you slow down, and your resistance to what is happening increases your perception of time. You think every second feels like an hour, and this is agonizing for many of you.

But does this mean that we can only shape time according to how we feel, and that if we want to speed time up or slow it down, we have to feel good or bad?

This is a good question, but it is not quite accurate in its assumption. You do not speed time up or slow it down according to your perception, but according to how you feel. You do not slow time down so that you can experience each second as a form of excruciating agony. No, the point is that your perception of time shifts according to your resistance to the moment. It is the resistance that allows you to see time differently. You can choose not to resist at all, and time will move quickly. But this is the paradox: The quick movement of time does not mean you are actually *present*. It means that you perceive each second without focus. You lose the perception of time because you are lost in a state of bliss—but that does not mean you are actually *present* in each second.

So how do you slow down or speed up time? It is not a question of removing resistance through pleasure, or increasing resistance through pain. We are not here to encourage you to speed time up by enjoying yourselves more, or slow it down by having a bad time.

No—the point is that your emotional state affects your ability to perceive time, and that is simply the measure of your ability to remain within the present moment, from moment to moment. So if you wish to be present, you will inevitably slow time down.

The issue is that you are not willing to be present in your lives. You do not wish to confront all that is going on, emotionally, and instead distract yourselves so that you can avoid the perception of time. Your perception of time—whether time appears to moving quickly or slowly—reflects how much you are resisting your experience of the present moment. Resistance is, for the majority of you, your typical emotional state. You do not wish to grapple with your resistance, so you look to distract yourself, because when you are in pain, time slows down.

So how can you be present without being in pain? You accept and do not resist what is there. Time is your friend; it is the measure of how present you are. Your willingness to be present in the moment—to be truly present, without any meaning attached—is what allows you to shift and expand or shrink time.

Your willingness to be present for your entire life, to be truly present to what is happening, is measured through your perception of time. You can slow time down by being entirely present to this second, and to the next one, and to the next one. And when you are not present to your life, it moves quickly, it speeds up. You lose your perception of time, and perceive time as moving quickly. In truth, it is because you are not at all present to each moment.

This is what happens when you numb and entertain yourselves to avoid the resistance you have to your true emotional lives. When you do that, time passes quickly. You have lots of fun, entertainment, etc., but are not fully present to what is occurring, and that keeps you from experiencing the resistance you have to the painful emotional underpinnings of your lives. And so you do not experience that pain—but you also don't experience presence. Time is simply the measure of how present you are in each second. It measures your perception, your awareness, of your life.

But you do not have to experience resistance to slow time down. That is simply the mechanism by which most of you do and can learn that you are able to slow time. Most of you slow time down when you stop resisting, and feel the pain of your life in the form of something anxious or dull or boring. But the truth is that you could experience pleasure or anything else in the exact same way if you were truly present. The stretching of time has nothing to do with having to experience pain or pleasure, but with your willingness to be present for each second in its fullness. How you experience that second may be through resistance or acceptance, and therefore through pain or pleasure. But if you wish to be fully present to that moment, you will ultimately just fully accept it, and experience that second completely. And you will then experience the slowing down of time.

2. Awakening to Your Divinity

To understand the path to the Christ Consciousness, to embrace your innate power to bend time, you must first understand your current relationship to the Divine. And so we must turn to the words *sacredness* and *sanctity*, which carry with them the history of your relationship to God. *Sacredness* suggests a space where God resides, where God is pure, and this space is untouched, holy, and has not been trampled upon with sin or dirt or whatever else you might use to describe the absence of God, the absence of purity. This concept speaks of a place where your thoughts are toward God and away from the mundane triviality of everyday life. *Sanctity*, too, suggests this, as if the space had been purified, cleansed, and left holy so that God could reside there untouched or unsullied by your negativity.

Sacredness and *sanctity* speak of the same thing, although the word *sanctity* also suggests that there is a place where only a few can go. So the words carry with them the connotations of God residing there, and of purity, but they also speak of a way of limiting, of keeping out, as if there were only a few sacred places, as if only a few could access the sanctified.

And this is the history of which we wish to speak: this history of access to the Divine. Because so many people believe that their connection is limited, and that only a few have it, many choose to disregard their own true access to the Divine. This history of your relationship to the Christ has been one in which only an anointed few have access to the sacred and sanctified realms of God. And you can reach those realms only through the priest or rabbi or another anointed figure.

And this has been a means of control, of the story of control. It has been a way to limit what people could do on their own. This is why the Buddha was actually such an important figure—because he opened up the authority of everyone's experience. So here, we tell you: Do not ask a priest, do not even ask the Buddha. Use your own experience as your guidepost.

Each and every one of you has access to the Divine at any time. Because you are Seeds of Light, you are slivers of the Creator, and so you do not need authority, you do not need permission, and you do not need anyone else to give you access. You do not need to believe anyone else who tells you that you have no authority. No, you may need another to help you access the Divine because you have been *taught* that you cannot access it, and do not know how to access it. But that is quite different from saying that you have to go through someone else because you do not have *permission* or are incapable—that you must rise to the hierarchy of the priest or the rabbi, and only then may you access God.

Rubbish.

You are all sacred, you are all sanctified in the sense that life, the energy of the Light, courses through you. But yes, you have accumulated a great deal of negativity; you have accumulated large amounts of karma and negative, bloated egos that do not allow you access. You deny *yourselves* access. It is not a question of the right permission from the right anointed figure, as if God put them on a list and said, *Talk only to them, otherwise I'm not here for you.* No, you do that with your egos, with the collective consciousness, which tells you that you are just bags of flesh walking around, consuming resources, and then you die. You deny your own access, you deny your own sacredness, and that is the history of your relationship to God. To continually deny, deny, deny your connection. And then you speak of God at moments of fear and terror, sometimes saying, *I don't often speak to you*, or, *If you're real, show yourself, and help me.* You turn to God in moments of crisis, and ask Him to save you when in fact you are always already connected to God.

Yes, if you cultivated it in times of love and peace and abundance, rather than in crisis, if you saw sacredness as something that was a part of your everyday lives, you would not need to call upon the Christ or turn to God at a moment of crisis, excusing your lack of attention. You would see that you have a connection to God at all times. You do not need an emissary, you do not need a go-between, except as a person who can teach you to find your own direct access, to undo the workings of the ego and put aside the beliefs, to get rid of the negativity that precludes your connection. Because it is not something you can call up like an emergency number. God is not a 9-1-1 distress signal.

Your sacredness and sanctity are to be cultivated and developed. When you do, you build up the relationship, the energetic connection, to the Divine, and you deepen your understanding of your place in this realm as a Seed of Light, as a sliver of the Creator. You cannot do this in an instant. You are not able to access this instantaneously through time, even though time, as we said, does not exist as you think it does.

But that is precisely the issue. It is as you think it is, and your thinking has been built up over time. You have a history of thought, about God, about your life, about who you are—and this is what must be unwound. This is what the authority, the teacher, provides: the ability to unwind the mind and the history of thought that keeps you separate from God, from the Light. You have a history of thought that says, *I am not sacred, I am not connected, only that priest or rabbi is*. And that is what must be undone.

∞

Your time has come to wake up and become who you truly are. You, as Seeds of Light, can expand and grow into great beams of Light, and can see beyond form, beyond the limitations that you impose on each other through your judgments and perceptions. You can recognize that you are infinite. You have no limitations other than those that you impose on yourself and others.

There is so much effort in your world at emancipation, at lifting up those who are otherwise subordinated or pushed down, and this we applaud—we applaud the effort to include—but it comes at a price. It comes at a price whereby you become attached to the very same forms that you would otherwise escape from if your attachment to them were not so strong. You would move beyond them and leave them behind, but you are so concerned with seeing the world through those forms that you cannot imagine a world *without* them; you cannot imagine being something *other* than a woman or man, or a gay or straight—whatever it is that you perceive yourself to be. And as we say, there is nothing wrong with these categories, because they are just a means of making yourself visible in a world that requires visibility.

But what if you imagined a world that did *not* require visibility in these forms? A world in which you could be anything and still be seen without reducing yourself to some sort of category?

But you do not imagine a world in which visibility is not tied to categories of identity. And so you replicate them in infinite ways, expanding those categories so that every product and everything that you buy, want, accumulate, or hold on to must somehow reflect this sense of a form to remain visible. You all understand the ways in which you do and do not participate in the categories that you identify with. Some of you try harder than others, but you all participate to some degree, and you are also aware of how far you are removed from those identities. Some women try to become as feminine as the collective consciousness holds possible, and so they buy things that are color-coded and gendered in a certain way, down to their purses or cell phone holders or anything else. And men do the same, as if they would suddenly cease to be alive if they were not somehow constantly upholding their form through the extension of their identity in the guise of objects and gadgets.

This is why the transgender is both a powerful movement, and something that will eventually be superseded. The idea that you are not limited by your corporeal body is an important understanding, and those who have incarnated as souls who adopt one identity and reside in the body of another are here to challenge the collective consciousness' perception of form. They will give way to those who live in one body and identify with another and yet do not seek alignment between the two, or others who do not identify with either. These categories will, as will all categories of form, eventually give way to visibility that does not require categories. It is inevitable, even if it will not take place in your lifetime.

Does the fact that there seems to be so much emphasis on this suggest that the forms are breaking down?

That is what happens. When older forms die, they do not go away easily; they struggle to maintain their life, their existence. Categories exist as part of the collective consciousness as energy, as energetic beings with their own lives, and you are seeing the death of identity forms in and around you. And the death of those forms, which is not their elimination but the shifting of their energy into a new form, requires that those energy forms give way to something else. They must stop existing at that frequency, and this, they will resist. They do not wish to be lifted up and transformed into something else. That energetic frequency seeks to continue as the energetic frequency it has always been. And so when categories of identity become testy and vocal and even violent, they are in fact trying to hold on to their frequency—to persist at this level of existence in this realm. And yet they, too, shall give way to something higher, to a different frequency. That is inevitable.

So do not regard this moment as one of failure or social collapse, where things are being broken down. No, this is a moment of ascension, when the forms of identity that have allowed you to be visible are being broken up and lifted, and yet are resisting. And that resistance makes them seem as if they were in need of protection, as the embattled. The battle over identity politics is not because there is a loss of emancipation. No, the true emancipation is unfolding. You will see this later, as other forms die away and you find yourself capable of being visible in new ways—ways you had not predicted or anticipated. Older forms will disappear, and you will no longer regard them with nostalgia or pain, as evidence of a better era. No, you will see them having given up their grip on this reality, as the energy shifts and transmutes to become something that has always been available, but has never become visible in this realm. The denseness is lifting, and so, too, are the limits on your potentiality.

3. Experiencing the Body Fully

The limits you impose on yourself begin, in the most simple of ways, with how you treat your body. Do you deprive yourself of the pleasures of eating certain foods? The choice to eat something like ice cream all too often becomes reduced to "good" or "bad," and is therefore not enjoyed properly. No, you do not fully embrace it and enjoy the sublime pleasure, the corporeal pleasure, that comes from consuming something like ice cream. And it need not be ice cream; it can be anything that you particularly enjoy. Maybe you enjoy it only sometimes, perhaps on special occasions, and you think something like, *Go ahead and sin just a little there, because you've earned it.*

Do you not see all the value judgments and morality bound up in something as simple as eating ice cream or whatever it is that you choose to eat? Rather than seeing it as a simple, divine pleasure that comes with inhabiting a human body, and that this is part of the reason for having a human body—to enjoy all the forms of physical pleasure—you make it a very complicated decision. Something that involves a matrix of good and bad: *And what about the effects on my body and weight?* or *Did I earn it?* or *Will it be from a cow that was well treated?* or *Does it harm the planet?*

Now, some of the considerations are valid. But you have complicated so much of your life with these sorts of questions, and taken away from the pure experience of pleasure. From the moment that the ice cream touches your lips, you are busy, busy, already calculating: *Well, I might have to spend an hour on the treadmill to overcome this extra weight gain,* and, *What if I get all congested or gassy from eating the dairy? Maybe I should stop at two spoonfuls,* and, *Oh, I never get to eat this,* and, *So I'm going to finish off the pint and then will just feel really bad about myself.* All of that emotional and mental baggage gets bound up in the pure experience of pleasure in the body.

You have the ability to be purely present to the pleasures of the body, in all of their forms, without binding them up in morality tales and considerations that may not be all that valid. We won't say that they don't have any validity, and we will address at another point how to take those into consideration, and what it means to choose to do something and why. But for now, we are focusing just on the choice: You have chosen to eat something that gives you enormous pleasure, but you don't enjoy it. Instead, you justify it, and rationalize it, and discuss it, and prepare to counteract it. Oh, and where did that pleasure go, buried beneath an avalanche of thoughts and worries about this simple choice? Not present at all, the experience of pleasure; it gets lost in the body when the mind takes over, and you don't experience the sublime quality of what the Divine has presented to you.

This is part of your lifestream: this simple, divine object of enjoyment. Do you know how you will enjoy ice cream when you are no longer in a body? You won't. You will enjoy other things and other manners of experiencing consciousness, to be sure, but you will not eat ice cream. So enjoy it, and take it for all it's worth, which is the utter, sublime gift of life that it is in that very moment. So simple, yet so full of grace. Do this with all that you enjoy, and just embrace it and honor it as the gift of love that it is. Do this with sex, do this with food, do this with massage, do this with any activity where your physical senses are activated and made to feel alive, because that is what is happening. Your senses are being activated with life; they are meant to do this, and this is what they are designed for: to experience the physical reality that is this realm in a way that cannot be experienced elsewhere in the same manner. This is the gift itself. So please do not labor over it when you have made the choice to experience physical pleasure in any form. Just experience it in its fullness.

∞

To experience the body fully you must confront the past that is carried in and through your physical form. This is a complicated topic, but we want to address it because it helps to explain why so many of you struggle with change, and with what you are, which is Light.

Your physical form is not the first physical form you've ever had. You've inhabited many physical forms in prior lifetimes. You have lived many lifetimes in many bodies, and most of you will never know the full extent of your past lives. That is okay. What is important to understand is that the memory of those past lives continues in your physical cells. It is held within the body, within the cellular structure itself, what you call DNA. How can it be otherwise? You came into being as a physical form, with a certain heritage, a lineage, of families that descended from others, and you are connected to those ancestors as well, and brought with you your own divine energy, your own spark of Light, that inhabits and animates this physical form, and which will leave this physical form at a future moment. So you bring this energy with you to each life, in and through the body, from your past and into the lifestream that you are currently experiencing as a physical form. So you have your childhood years, and your infancy in the womb, and all of the previous lifetimes of energy bound up in a single form. That is the collective energy of your soul, of your Seed of Light, animating this physical form.

Do you ever wonder why you have certain predilections or interests, or certain fears or illnesses? Not everything can be explained by your connection with your parents, though much can. No, some of this will be energy from lifetimes ago. And so many of you have some sort of fear or limitation or belief that comes from a past lifetime, where you experienced energy of a particular vibration, of a particular frequency, and you carry that energy with you until you resolve it—or until you decide not to create it anew. This is the learning process of the soul. You will carry that energy with you and continue to reproduce it until you can release it and stop producing it. That is karma.

Your cells contain that energy, and that is why you manifest certain illnesses or patterns, or why your body is good at some things and not others. Some of you like to dance or have patchy skin or have certain pigmentation, and others have specks of color in their eyes, and some have problems with their nails. All of these are just physical expressions of your energy. And certain wavelengths come up for examination and resolution. And that is why you often experience so much in and through the physical form—because that physical form is the expression of that energy, and it will come in through illness, especially, to be resolved.

This is why illness and injury are not to be regarded as failings. No—these are moments where the physical form comes under attack and requires special care and attention, but this is not a failing. It is not an event that you lament as having been your "fault." This is the emergence of energy that your soul never resolved, and that now requires resolution as part of your evolution. So, much like the pleasure that you experience in the body, when the cellular memories of your previous lifetimes come forward to be heard and addressed, often but not always through illness or injury, you must meet them with love, and embrace them just as you would ice cream or any other physical pleasure. It may not seem pleasurable, but it is the same relationship to the body: the gift of life coming forward to be met with full presence. And so you meet that energy that wasn't resolved in a past lifetime or in your childhood, and when you meet it with full love and presence, it can be resolved and cleared. Then you will see the immense power and pleasure that comes from your physical form, of experiencing your physical form fully and completely, whether it is through pleasure or pain.

4. Seeing Each Other Anew

As a spark of the Creator, who has inhabited lifetimes of physical bodies carrying lifetimes of memories, how do you now re-create yourself in the image of the Christ? We are here to teach you how. But first, some basic points are necessary, so that you can understand what we're saying. This is a reprisal of our past teachings.

∞

You are a Seed of Light. You are both *in* time and space and *out* of time and space. In this realm, you experience time and space as part of your agreement with others. You must understand that you re-create yourself from second to second, and that at each instant, the past drops away, so that you only experience the present. But your present is often focused on what is to come or what has already passed, and so you rarely actually inhabit the gift of life that is the present moment. You experience instead the present as a re-creation of the past, or a projection of the past into the future, and in so doing, do not ever feel the full bliss of the second that you are now experiencing. Here and here, and again and again. And when you meet others, you do not see them as the instant re-creations they are. You see them not in their resurrected forms, or as what they are in that second, but as your memory of them—how they appeared to you in a past moment. And you anticipate that they will reappear to you again in the future, in the same way. And for some, that is the case, but most people have changed, even imperceptibly, though you do not acknowledge that.

This leads us to the crux of this teaching, which is that when you meet someone you have met in the past, there are not two people. No—there is a relationship, an energetic creation that is separate and connected with each of you as Seeds of Light. That is, your Seeds of Light come together in a manner that reflects a certain vibrational frequency—an energy that was once created. Because you resurrect each other in the forms of the past, you sometimes resurrect each other in ways that are no longer true. Have you noticed that when you return home to your families, you act in ways that reflect how you were years ago? Or when you meet someone from college, you exhibit older forms of speech or behavior, which you have long abandoned? Yes, the relationship that emerges with you is its own entity; it has its own energy field and vibration, and so you have to learn that when you are in a relationship with each other, you are constantly re-creating each other in that instance. And so your co-creation of the world depends on your ability to re-create yourself in the now, in the present moment, rather than in the past, with this person for whom you only exist as a vestige of the past, as a ghost.

So how do you shift so that you do not appear in the same way or fall into the energetic signature of a past relationship? You begin by acknowledging that you are showing up believing that the other person is just as you remember, and understanding that you are resurrecting them as a past version, not as the present version of who they are. Can you shift your view and see this person anew—not as a simulacrum of the past, of some memory, but with fresh eyes? Can you hold the memory of who they were, and yet still meet them fully in the present, as someone who was once connected to you and is now different, in ways that you cannot yet imagine or appreciate?

You can shift the dynamic of the relationship by meeting this person in the now, in the moment, in this very second, without projecting onto them any expectation that they conform to the image you forged years ago, or even just yesterday. In this way, you create a relationship that is new. For this is what you do to each other: You co-create each other in the present moment based on the past, and therefore tie each other to versions of your past selves. This is a form of control and emotional bondage, as you tie the person to a representation that no longer exists. How painfully limiting, for your power to create and re-create yourselves is, as we have said, the gift of being human and a Seed of Light in this realm. Yes, *you* can create yourself anew, but because you are always in an act of co-creation, *others* create you as you once were. So you must meet each other in the present, not in the past. Meet each other with an appreciation of the past, but then let it go. That is how a new entity is formed, a new relationship, and it will have a different signature.

This is the key to reforming your lives—by beginning to rebuild and find relationships based on the present moment, based on who you are now. And this process never ends; you are constantly changing, lifting, and uplifting, as you access your higher self, and the Christ Consciousness begins to deepen within you. This means that you are in connection with others in ways that are constantly in flux, never static, and never fixed. Does this make it hard to maintain social relationships? Only when someone expects you to be who you were yesterday or a second ago, or a year ago, and finds that you are not. But if you both show up and co-create with the other as equally divine creations in the present moment, then no. You will meet each other where you are. And that means that your relationships will deepen and grow and shift over time as *you* grow and shift over time. You will not resurrect the dead. That is what you do now, and you find it exhausting and debilitating to be captive to what you once were. To change, you must stop seeing the other as a reflection of your mental images from the past, and see them anew, with fresh eyes.

Is there some worry that you won't be able to maintain connections because you will be changing? No—your changes, when part of your growth and ascension toward your higher self, do not mean that you are entirely erratic, that from one second to the next you become an entirely different person with no connection to anything with which you might have identified before. You're not shape-shifting or deciding that you only eat this kind of food today and this kind of food tomorrow, or changing your language or speech patterns. We mean instead that your relationship to your higher self, and to all others, changes, and this fundamental change means that you drop the baggage of the past that you had carried with you—or re-created in each second. Instead, you say, *Who is this divine Seed of Light who shows up before me? Yes, I recognize that this is someone I have known for a long time. Yes, I know their history, but who are they today, right now, in this instance?* You do not say, *Well, so-and-so always says and does this, so I'm going to assume that so-and-so will do this*. Instead, you will see each other as perfect strangers that you have known for some time. Can you understand the paradox? You approach them from a place of inquiry and welcome, not suspicion, not asking yourself, *Who is this stranger whom I don't know and might harm me?* Instead: *Who is this person today, what new aspect of their lifestream is going to unfold before my very eyes?*

That is the wonder and love you will begin to see in the relationships you have with other people. You can go into a relationship with the same curiosity and openness that comes with not knowing someone already.

∞

Your inability to approach others with wonder, curiosity, and openness means that many of you struggle with intimacy—with being seen and seeing the other person. And this is okay. There is nothing wrong with that struggle. Allay your fears that there is something wrong with you. You struggle with intimacy because you fear that you will be rejected, and you believe this in part because you reject others. Yes, you know that if people reveal aspects of themselves that you do not like, or that do not comport with your views, you will reject them. Sometimes outright, sometimes subtly, sometimes by simply slipping away and allowing the relationship to die, like a grape on a vine. And so this is what you expect from others as well, as you mirror each others' consciousness. You fear that showing yourself will lead to rejection.

So how do you move beyond this impasse? You cannot move beyond it. For there *is* no impasse; there is only your belief that you cannot share yourself with another. If you share yourself with another, and the other person rejects you, you regard that as confirmation of your lack of lovability. Instead, you must begin by sharing yourself, wholly and fully, without fear of abandonment, without fear of retribution, and without fear of loss. For if you "lose" someone, it only means that the other person has left your lifestream. It doesn't mean anything about your worth. That is the meaning you create, and it is not true. It is a claim to unworthiness that you do not need to make; it is a statement of value that you do not have to declare. Make no such declaration. The only declaration is the truth of what you have seen and experienced, which is the authentic sharing of one's self, and the other person's experiencing that and reacting to it. If that person is fully present, if that person actually feels your authenticity, then they will be moved.

This is the movement beyond the supposed impasse, and it allows the other person to relinquish their own fear of rejection at the same time. And so the two of you come together, co-creating each other in and through authenticity, re-creating each other in a shared space of openness and intimacy. This is what intimacy is: the sharing of one's self without fear of the consequences that might unfold.

Do you realize how little you share with each other? You share only each other's simulacra—visions of what you think the other person must want to see to be loved and accepted. How impoverishing is this for you? You know that there is a core that wants to be let outside, and yet you hide behind thin veils. Why, we ask, when the power of your truth is so much more delightful than any pretense or mirage?

With this intimacy, you can begin to co-create each other as equals, as authentic beings whose cores are ready to be shared with others. This is what you must do with each other as you begin to embody the Christ Consciousness. You must allow yourselves to share your authentic selves with each other, rather than the fable you present as an acceptable image for the rest of the world to consume. No, you must be authentic in all situations, with all people, for that presence will change and alter your relationships so fundamentally that you will not be able to imagine what it is like to connect with others at any other level. Instead, you connect now through your images, through your mirages, and only imagine what would happen if you were to share yourself fully and authentically.

And that is almost always a tale of fear, a narrative of rejection and abandonment, or at least some sort of conflict or division between you and other people. The relationship will be cleaved in advance by this assumption, so that you will compartmentalize and split yourself, a part of you never making itself present or part of the conversation. Again, how limiting and how impoverishing.

We say that this is not the way to be intimate with one another.

Intimacy is the sharing of yourself, and in that full presence, the power of that presence will allow the other person to be present as well. The fear will drop away, and you will see the other person as an equally divine creation that you have never seen before. You will begin to see the other person as *their* truth, which you have not seen yet, and will realize that your fear is a result of you judging yourself through the eyes of that other person's mirage. You projected your own fear in and through that other person.

What would the simulacrum of my friend say about my truth?

This is what you ask yourself, and this means two mirages, two false images, are speaking to each other. Drop them and see each other for real. And then decide if you are meant to intertwine your lifestreams. Maybe you aren't. But that means your relationship was never authentic, never intimate, and there was only the illusion of connection, the two of you seeking something that wasn't there. In almost all cases, the power of your presence will forge a new connection, something more powerful than you could imagine. And if the other person cannot share their authenticity, if their entrapment by the ego is so strong that they remain attached to their mirage, then so be it. That is not your place to judge; it is not your place to worry about their role in your life. They are there for a reason: for you to mirror back their authenticity through your own. And once you have done that, your relationship is complete. How that unfolds and whether your lifestream leads you away from or closer to this person is not for you to decide. That is the power of intimacy: to allow yourself to be led by your truth to those who would mirror it back to you, so that you may see yourself and others as divine creations.

∞

To speak of intimacy and how you share yourself with another is also to speak of *discourse* and *intercourse*—*discourse*, for the language that you use to describe the ways you talk about particular things, and *intercourse*, which suggests procreation and something biological. There is no difference between these words. Discourse and intercourse between two or more people is in fact production and creation, at the level of the word, as a form of creative production and recreation. The energy of your words creates your reality, and so you are in fact engaging in intercourse when you engage in discourse.

The intercourse that you primarily engage in is not the biological one; no, it is the discursive one, where you generate your reality between two people, which creates more realities between groups of people, and between all people. You create through language. The words you use to describe your world are in fact the creation of it. Imagine the infant who stares at the world and sees only blurry shapes and forms. They do not know what they see, and yet they see much more than you do. And as they move ever further from God, they see less and less, as they are absorbed into the collective consciousness.

Your vocabulary limits you, shapes you, defines you in so many ways, from the words you use to talk about yourselves—identity words and categories—to all other forms of unifying yourself in and through language. You do this all the time, and in so doing you limit yourselves. And so you limit your ability to create, because you develop relationships with each other through the same language again and again. There are shifts, there are openings, and this is wonderful. We love seeing the many possibilities in and through language as you expand your concept of what it means to be human, of what it means to occupy a human body in this plane. Yes, through your intercourse you can create anew through language. So why do you limit your re-creations, and why do you choose to repeat yourself again and again in the same ways?

Understand that this creation is actually a product of your discourse, a product of your language. You invent something that you already have words for. But what do you do to create things for which you have *no words*? When using your creative faculties to generate your world, you cannot create something new through the mind's expectations. Because there are phenomena that are not yet part of your experience, and not yet part of your consciousness, and therefore not yet part of your language. So you must bypass the mind to experience something that you have no words for, though you may come up with words to describe it later. And doing so will allow you to replicate and reproduce this new experience within your language.

Each of you has new experiences, but you reduce them to versions of things that you experienced before, and make them therefore less radical, less powerful—all because you do not have the ability to explain them. And this is the part where you grow, because if you do not have words for an experience, it means you have experienced something truly new—not the replication of something you had already experienced, in a new form, like a change of outfit. No, this is where your mental framework for future possibilities in relationships and reality shifts to allow for more and more.

Your relationships are often a source of support, but they are equally a source of replication and reduction, as we have seen. And this is not a criticism of your connections, but only to say that you have a tendency to reproduce yourselves in discourse, through the intercourse of language, through the same speech and words again and again. What are your conversations with people, how do you describe the relationships you have, and what words do you exchange? These are what make your relationships; the words you use generate the energy that exists between you and those who come into your lifestream. You connect through the energy of the words that you use. What is the energy of your relationships? Does it have a lot of anger? Is your language rooted in fear? Look at the words you use, and they will show you what you are creating, in and through discourse, each and every day.

We challenge you to look at your creations, and how you co-create each other in and through language. We have spoken of how you met each other in the past, in forms that you already understood, when the person had actually changed and is no longer the person you met yesterday or even an hour ago. And yet you insist on shaping each other—and the relationship between you—based on the past, and this is the crux of our teaching. The relationships you form and continue to produce and create between you mark how you are creating in and through language.

You each may have changed, but you meet each other as mirages, and through those mirages generate a relationship, with its own life form and energy. And that life form is constructed in and through the words and language you choose. And when you have changed and grown and altered, you may find that the relationship becomes a sort of straightjacket. You cannot abide its energy; the words you used in the past to build that relationship no longer fit your *present* emotional and energetic state, because you have changed the energy of the words that you would use to describe yourself and the world. You no longer wish to co-create in the same way, and the relationship feels off.

This is where your authenticity must come through, so that you can co-create each other and the relationship in a new language, at a higher vibration than you have achieved before, so that the relationship will be at the vibration where you currently are. This is why relationships must continue to grow beyond the past, beyond the mirages that you once had of each other.

5. Blasphemy of Others

Blasphemy further speaks to how you relate to each other. And blasphemy is not some blind adherence to a dogma that you reject only when it does not suit your purposes. It is instead the situation when you do not see reality for what it is, and yet you speak as if you knew. This is turning your back on reality, turning your back on the truth. And we are here today to discuss the ways in which you blaspheme *each other*.

Yes, we are using this heavy word to talk about your treatment of each other. You do not see one another as divine creatures, and you do not see each others' truth. Instead, you speak of one another in ways that do not reflect that truth—and that speech is blasphemy. You blaspheme other people by tying them to the past, to some version of themselves that once existed—or never existed and was just your projection of who they were—and so you go around talking about this person as if you knew their truth, as if your words could incarnate them in the truth as you see it. This is blasphemy.

We are not talking just about how you see the person. We are talking about how you speak of them to others, in other contexts, and how this creates an image of the person through the energy of your words. Because, as you know, you are all co-creating each other in the now, in the present moment, and doing so with your words. If you co-create someone else, not according to their truth but according to your projections and fears and misbeliefs, you blaspheme them, you deny their truth, and you deny their status as a divine being. This is what you do with your social media, or when you complain about someone else. You have spent much of your time actually generating each other, and in doing so you perpetuate your misunderstandings of each other. For you alter the collective understanding of them, and that affects them in myriad ways. The words you use are creative and have force; they contain energy, and in using them you build the person up to be a certain way through the images that you generate.

No, we are not speaking of defamation or telling mistruths in a legal sense. We are speaking of the ways you generate each other through your descriptions of how others behave, through your opinions, through retelling and gossip, all said in ways that do little to perpetuate the truth of who they are at their core. Yet you feel entitled to speak with such authority about their lives, based on the most trivial of connections, bypassing them in just seconds. And in that second you take it upon yourself to co-create them in the future according to this perception, and this is what you must stop doing. You must stop blaspheming each other.

Instead, recognize the limits of what you know about each other, until you show up and make yourself present, and then, when you speak about others, adhere to the experience that you have had, with full awareness of who you were at that moment. Yes, it sounds complicated, but it isn't. Instead of saying, "So-and-so was mean to me. Can you believe what she did?" over and over until you and others have come to an agreement about the status of this person as a mean person, you can simply explore what it is that she said to you that caused you to feel such pain.

And instead of recalling and perpetuating the harm by speaking negatively, instead of giving voice to your wound, you can simply explore it and say, in a more objective way, "This is what someone said to me. To be honest, I felt pain when I heard that. I wonder why." Do you need to demonize the person to explore what that encounter meant for your lifestream? No, not at all, because you co-created him or her, and that experience, at that very moment, so you must look at *yourself* as the source of that encounter. Yes, you must look inside, at your feelings, to understand what part of you was seeking expression, what part of you had been reincarnated at that moment in that encounter to be expressed. There you must go—not to the demonization of the other person by creating an image of him or her that fits your liking. No, you do not know what transpired for that person. So let him or her be.

You do this with all sorts of people—in fact, with everyone. Much of your dialogue is composed of talking about others in ways that blaspheme them and do not honor them as Seeds of Light, do not honor the ways in which they, too, are divine creatures. So do not blaspheme. Do not spend your time online and on social media simply speaking ill of others because it suits some emotional wound that you feel needs expression. Recognize that you blaspheme, and explore instead. Otherwise, you do this person great harm; you generate energy around them that they then have to contend with, and which affects them in a myriad of ways that you cannot see or anticipate. You cannot tell what karmic effects your words will have on that person, so you must watch those words and speak only of your experience with them, and reflect on your feelings, and your role in co-creating your experience.

Can you elaborate on this?

Yes. The people who occupy your public eye bear enormous amounts of energy that you do not, because you live a relatively private life by comparison. Yet the amount of energy that is conveyed in and through your words when you construct them as certain people, as either good or bad, or honest or dishonest, or talented or not—these all have effects on their lives. And not just because those words may influence others, although that is significant. If you say that so-and-so should not get a role, should not be elected, should not play that sport, should not be on television, others may agree, and this may lead to consequences. But even the utterance of those words, due to their negativity, has an effect on those people and their energetic field. You connect to them and co-create them in that moment, and so you are in fact affecting their lives.

This is why the Buddhists emphasize right speech. The effects of the words, the energy they contain, is a form of creation, because language is the bridge by which you mediate separation. This means, as we have already seen, that you co-create each other in and through your words. Recognize your power and do not blaspheme each other, for if you were to regard each person as the Seed of Light that they are, as a divine creation, as a spark of the Creator's vision, how could you but marvel at their majestic role in creating the fabric of the universe as it currently exists? For you do not know the roles that they play in the lives of many people. Honor that and be humble in the face of their brilliance, so that they, too, might honor you and be humble before *your* brilliance.

6. Our Relationship with Our Mothers

At the core of your relationships, and how you co-create each other, is the figure of the mother, for it is around the mother that there is so much energy, and so much division. There is much to be said about your relationship with your mother. Yes, she is a singular creation, for she is the portal through which you came into this realm, both literally and figuratively, as you passed through the birth canal and entered into a form separate and apart from hers. And this was the first division—from the union that existed prior to that birthing moment. And at the same time, it was a figurative birth, insofar as you entered this realm connected to your birth mother's lineage and history, and from there you developed much of your understanding of what it means to be human.

Yes, the relationship with the mother is fundamental; not the whole picture, to be sure, but it sets a foundation, and many of you continue to play out your relationship with your mother in many other contexts. And so we want to explore how you ought to relate to your mother in and through the Christ Consciousness.

Understand, first and foremost, that without your mother, you would not have life; it is the single most important fact, and is the basic premise of your very existence in form, as a physical manifestation of a Seed of Light. And that is no small undertaking. Therefore, you can always recall this as a way to think about your mother and co-create her as an angelic being—yes, an angelic being. Angels move between the physical and the nonphysical in ways that other beings do not, as others may only operate in the realm of the energetic, and in other dimensions, but not in the physical realm. So yes, your mothers are angelic, for they too traverse the line between the physical and the nonphysical, and thus allow you to become part of this realm. And this is a wonderful thing to applaud.

But most of you struggle, most of you wonder, *Why is my mother not like other mothers? Why is she not like Mary?* Or, *Why is she not like a goddess or a Divine Mother or even just like my aunt or grandmother? Why is my mother filled with such baggage?* Yes, your mothers have their "baggage," and they pass it along to you. It is your inheritance, and your debt to them, to carry their emotional baggage, their karma. Your mothers pass to you their energetic expressions that they themselves have continued to reproduce lifetime after lifetime, and you take those on as part of your heritage, as part of your lineage in and through the mother.

The mother's lineage is especially powerful because it is associated with the creation of life in physical form. So many of you feel a strong bond to your mother, and even if you feel an intense or strong hatred, the bond is strong. For many of you, your bond with your father is less strong. And the bond with the mother requires you to address and grapple with that karmic debt, which is the emotional and energetic baggage. You model all of your relationships with each other, with the world, through the eyes of your mother.

The child inherits and takes on the ways that the mother sees the world, in order to be the recipient of the mother's love. And this sets up a paradigm for all other relationships. No doubt you notice as you become older that you start to resemble your mother. Some of you do not, because you have rejected your mothers or identified more with your fathers—and that's okay, we'll address that later. But you must begin to co-create by looking carefully at the energetic inheritance from your mother, and forgiving her for what you have taken on, for she did not know what she was doing. How could she? She is a divine creation, a Seed of Light, but she is not a Divine Mother in the sense that she knows the full truth of who she is. No, she was stuck in the realm of separation, just like you, and carried all manner of energetic expressions from the collective consciousness about who to be and what to say, and who had worth and who didn't. And this in turn included what it meant to love and be loved, and what requirements were attached to love.

And this is the fundamental point: You all believe that love comes with requirements—for giving it *and* for receiving it. For it to be love, true love, it must have all of these requirements attached to it, as if they would certify it as authentic love. And that certification comes directly from your mother. So if you want to understand how it is that you relate to people the way you do, and co-create them as such, then you must look at the ways you and your mother co-created each other. Once you do, you will forgive her, because this is not a question of blame. No, this is a question of co-creation, of seeing each of you as you are. And this is what you have agreed to by coming into form in and through this particular mother in this particular moment in time and space, and that is your obligation. Your goal, your purpose in waking up, is to address how you relate to your mother. That is why there are so many jokes in spiritual communities about how you can be enlightened, except around your mother. It is the fundamental relationship that shapes your entire framework for relating to and managing separation.

How do you analyze your relationship to your mother? Begin

by seeing exactly where you feel pain, exactly where you feel that your mother doesn't love you, or what the requirements are for love, and then see where else in your life you have replicated those requirements, attaching them as conditions to those around you—to your work, friendships, partners, husbands, wives, children, and everything else. It all comes back to your mother.

7. The Role of the Father

We have spoken of your relationship to the mother as your primordial model for relationships, and how that shapes much of your relationship with the rest of the world. Now we wish to speak of fathers, and the role of the father.

There is nothing essential about the role of the mother and females, except for the one key fact that it does requires a female to give birth, and that birthing is significant. It is the gift of life itself. And so there is a difference between mothers and fathers, which is that the role of the mother can never fully be played by a male figure, while the role of the father *can* be played by a female figure.

We are here to speak of the *role* of the father, and for now we will assume the role of the father is male, since that still applies to the majority of you, despite a lack of essential requirement that the father be male. The father figure takes on such essential meaning for so many of you. And for Patrick, the father figure was deeply misunderstood, deeply disconnected—and many of you have that same relationship, with the disconnection of the father, the absence of the father from your life. While many of you struggle with your mothers, that was at least a place of a great deal of emotional energy. The father all too often presents the opposite, which is to say, the absence of emotional energy.

In this way, the father captures the essential aspect of separation in a way that the mother, with whom you were physically one at one point, does not. For the father was always separate from you as you came into form. The father was someone who supplied a part that you integrated and were born from, but you were one with the mother, while the father was always separate. And it is this primordial difference that shapes your understanding of fathers, and how you relate to them.

It is not a requirement that the father be symbolic of this separation. You have assumed that physical reality—that your father was separate from you while you were one with your mother—means that you must necessarily be separated emotionally from your fathers. This idea infiltrates so many of your relationships with your fathers. It is important that we address this, because while you learn certain models of relationships with your mother, in other words you embrace her views on separation, you must understand that separation itself comes from your belief that the father was separate from you. Yes, you learn separation as a structure from the father, first—not from the mother. And so it is this constant separation from the father that influences your belief that separation is real.

Your relationship with your mother models for you how to connect emotionally, and is often the source of tremendous difficulty, because of the ways in which you learned all manner of emotional beliefs from your mother. It is the mother who conveys her family's karma regarding beliefs and unworthiness, and those are carried to male and female children alike. But it is the father who teaches you the structure of separation, and the belief in separation itself. To put it differently, if you were once tied to your mother but never to your father, it stands to reason that for the small child, there is always separation, and the belief that the connection with its mother was illusory and can never be regained. The child therefore thinks that there are some people with whom they will never be one, and can never be one.

That is, the father teaches you that this separation is the truth of this realm, and that you are separate from all others. This is why so many people have a bond with their mothers, and replicate that bond with their mothers, but struggle with their father. For it is the father who teaches you not to show emotion, and that there is no need for emotion. So you learn to bond emotionally via the mother, but associate the father with emotional separation.

And so it is essential to make peace and forgive your fathers, because many of you simply dismiss them, write them off, abandon them, and think, *I'll focus on my mother, my father was never really a part of my life, he wasn't emotionally available.* And this is the fundamental structure lying beneath your relationship with all others, on top of which you layer the emotional bonds that you learned from your mother. Now, this is not always the case; there are examples where fathers acted more like mothers, and vice-versa. Understand that we speak of the *tendencies* of humans to learn their relationships from the models presented to them, and this is the fundamental structure. This is how you learn to relate to each other in time and space, having forgotten your status as Seeds of Light.

∞

Now we must talk about the emotional importance of the father, who stands as the figure of separation. The father figure is the one that lays down rules, and often lays down very strong dictates about how to behave. That is, the father elaborates on the structures of separation, and how society has developed through that separation. The father will tell you when to sleep and eat, when to leave and come home, etc. And the father is typically associated with punishment and with ensuring order. That is, the father exists to manage and maintain unity within separation, to allow for the flow even though separation is inherent.

What is ironic is that when men actually become fathers, they all too often experience the type of unconditional love that is irreconcilable with separation, which calls into question separation itself. It is not uncommon for new fathers to explain that being a father has changed their view of the world—but that is not entirely true. Those individuals have always perceived something else, something more, which is partly what led them to become fathers in the first place. And for many of them, there is something so overwhelming about it that they entrench themselves even more deeply in separation. From their experience of unconditional love they do not learn that there is no separation. No, instead, they believe that separation, or rather the means and rules and laws that govern separation, are absolutely necessary to guarantee the survival of the child, this newfound source of unconditional love. And so the father entrenches himself in the norms and mores of his society, of the collective consciousness of separation, out of an instinct to protect and ensure the child's survival. The father does not conclude that the world is actually perfect as it is, and that the child is protected at all times, and that he is misperceiving what he assumes to be threats to the child. No, he takes on the role of the savior, which would not be necessary outside the realm of separation.

The father's preoccupation with this type of survival, with its rules and norms of separation in the collective consciousness, means that he abdicates the emotional expression of love that often accompanies relationships. Not all fathers, to be sure, but many. That is why you have a stereotypical image of a father who is emotionally absent and abdicates the emotional connection to the mother. You have fathers who *do* express emotion, but they do not associate it with their role of being a father. They associate it with something else. When called upon to fulfill their role as father, they necessarily turn to the structures of separation and say, you must manage yourself this way, you must negotiate with life in that way, this is what it means to be an adult in this realm. And so they continue to enforce through laws and norms of separation.

But there is a point of intersection where masculinity and fatherhood merge, and that is where the father associates his expression of emotion as something not fully masculine—as something of a departure from his normal male self—and where the father figure, the role of the father, both permits and circumscribes it. For the father is *supposed* to love his child, and that love takes the form of always being ready to assist and provide and be there to explain and make the child feel protected. Where the mother comforts, the father protects. That is their way. It is not the way for every single mother and father, but these are the structures and roles you have laid out and identified for yourselves, and even when you challenge them, you challenge them because they have been installed and agreed upon as part of the collective consciousness as the roles of the mother and father. The father understands that his emotional outpouring is meant to take a certain form, and so the father figure is both permission and limitation on the expression that the father, the male figure, might offer his child.

This is both beneficial and limiting, insofar as it means that the emotional expression of love that you are all capable of, separate and apart from the gendered norms that you have embraced to govern your interactions, is available to anyone outside of any role. Why should the father figure *not* be allowed the full range of expression of love? We say that it is absurd, because you have decided to limit love, to channel it along certain currents, in the name of a role that anyone can adopt.

And this is how you go ahead and break out of it. Do not say that to be a father means that you must reiterate and protect in and through the collective consciousness as it exists. Do not regard the father as the protector of the norms and laws of separation, so that the child might survive. Regard the child as the divine creation itself, and extend it love, and see that you are capable of providing any and all necessary types of love. You do not need to be limited. The result is that your child will not see you as limited, either, and will not see the father as emotionally withdrawn, having abdicated that role to the mother. The father *can* love—and love in ways that you do not currently allow. This limitation on the role of the father is not accurate, for he can love just like the ultimate Father from whom you have sprung, the Divine Father—that figure who loves without any need to reflect or limit that love to a certain type.

∞

The role of the father is directly related to how you regard your model of masculinity and emotional availability. You wonder why the father figure is about separation, yet you understand perfectly that the father is also the figure who represents what an ideal male should be in your world. That is why fatherhood is so idealized, and why you regard the father with such reverence. And this model of masculinity is tied to the absence of emotion, because it is tied to the caretaker and provider and survival mechanism that you also believe you must have.

All male figures relate to the father figure in some way or another, even if they do not have a father present in their lives, and do not have any desire or plan to become a father themselves. The father figure nevertheless weighs heavily, casts a shadow you might say, on what it means to be a man in this world. And that does not mean that all men relate in the same way, or that only men relate to the father figure. But this is the binary relationship you have all formed so that you divide the world into male and female. Even when you try to blur this distinction, you are still nevertheless operating with these two poles. You are either man or woman. There is, in your world, no true third option, but only a deviation from those two poles. That is how you have constructed yourselves.

As we have said, the father figure, who represents the structure of separation and the survival mechanism or caretaker, does not have to be a man. Nevertheless, the father figure is important for how you all relate to gender, and particularly how men relate to the father figure and to masculinity. Many of you struggle with why men do certain things, like kill and steal, and so many men are responsible for so much death and destruction, and you might think that this is a requirement for men—that to be a man, one must plunder and murder and wage war. And you play this dynamic out in many ways, through sports and games and other activities where men get to play the role of fighter, warrior, and murderer in contexts that do not actually deprive humans of life, but reflect the fundamental figure of the male as such.

How does this relate to the father?

The father figure, as we have said, is the figure that presents the structure of separation, which means that the father figure presents the possibility that you will be separate from all other objects. The father establishes this structure, and therefore you learn, via that figure, that objects are separate from you, and that you are therefore separate from them. And that is the basis for your existence. You are not those things. You are not your father, and your father is not you, and never was, unlike the mother. So there is a fundamental separation between you and others, and the male who becomes a father believes that to survive, to take care of those objects that are separate from him but necessarily linked via his genetics, he must engage in certain activities to protect and defend those objects. Because they are separate from him and all else, they are fragile, vulnerable, and subject to removal from this physical plane. In other words, they may die.

That is the fundamental belief of separation: that because you exist separately from those objects, you may also not be a part of those objects … and can therefore be removed. So the father figure becomes the figure who protects and defends those objects—his children—from those threats. That is why the father associates masculinity with fighting, war, etc.

I admit that I'm having a hard time accepting all of this, because this seems a bit pat, a bit easy, and it also ignores how much mothers can be protectors of their children.

You and your brethren believe that you've unraveled something so thorny and complex in life. It's as if you needed complexity to make it seem like understanding gender was worth the effort. But the fact remains that your parents are your main templates for your relationship to physical reality and to gender, and this has not changed in millennia. It is the simple truth. And so while you might come up with very sophisticated analyses that purport to capture how the brain identifies with others, as well as complex charts and very arcane terminology to explain gender, it need not be that hard to understand.

What we wish to impress upon you is the idea that the father captures the sense of emotional vulnerability as survivalist vulnerability. That is, the father does not show emotion, because the father as caretaker is protecting against the threat to one's survival, and therefore it is the mother who comes to embody the expression of emotion. And so you replicate those patterns again and again, and this is why the same issues occur throughout a lineage, and why people exclaim, "Oh, I'm becoming my mother!" Or, "I'm just like my father!" Yes, this is what you do: You become your parents, and you relate to others through the same lenses.

You do not need a complicated theory of how gender norms are replicated to understand that the trauma of being a human being stems in part from the models of separation that you receive from your parents. Of course, there are exceptions and different models, and we do not mean to suggest that this paradigm is precisely the same for everyone, but that's what makes it a paradigm. There are exceptions.

But for those who wish to understand the role of fathers and the relationship to masculinity, it is important to understand why the masculine figure is not permitted the same range of expression, the same emotional output as others are afforded. Even when boys are younger and given an opportunity, it is conveyed to them, through the collective consciousness, that this is a stage they will have to give up. They are told that they cannot cry when they are adult males, and they cannot show sensitivity or vulnerability in the same way. No, they must prepare for the inevitable fight—the warfare that is required for surviving in this physical world. That is the story that you tell each other, again and again and again. The result is that there are those who struggle mightily with the expectations imposed on them by the father figure as the model of masculinity, as the one who takes care of others and does not suffer or show emotions, who survives and fights, and occasionally thrives.

That is your model, and even the most sensitive father still has a limited range of emotion. For those who are not able to live up to this, it can be crushing, a veritable mockery of their claim to existence in this realm. For you—and by "you," we mean the collective consciousness—tell them that they are not who they think they are, that they are not a full man or even a partial man, and cannot lay claim to that identity because they do not satisfy its requirements, which go well beyond the mere physical form and genitalia. No, they cannot live up to the role that the collective consciousness demands of them, and eventually this causes such grief and pain that they seek power. They take up war against their fellow man in a way that will vindicate their sense of power, that will show others they can fight, that they are in fact "men."

This is what occurs again and again, in small ways and in large disasters. And you sit around and wonder, are they mentally ill? Are they somehow disturbed? No—not in the way that you might think. You are all mentally ill in this way, which is to say that you all impose on each other a burden based on a misguided view of what reality is, and therefore impose on each other certain types of identities and ranges of emotional expression that do not reflect your full potential, or your status as human beings with every emotion available to you. You are Seeds of Light who have infinite potential, and yet you limit yourselves and others so much in the process of conforming to what the collective consciousness demands of you. And when you cannot conform, you are cast out, your claim to existence does not hold. That is the message given to those who are wounded again and again, until they cannot take it anymore and lash out in violent and horrific manners. And you wonder whether they are sick.

No—they are the collective creation of all of you. They are your children, and you are their father. You have given birth to them when you collectively generated the circumstances that gave rise to an individual's violent outburst and backlash against a system that told him, *You do not exist.* It is your own delusion that creates this situation. You create the child; you father him by telling him that he is separate from you, and that to be with you, he must act in this way, and if he doesn't, it will mean that he doesn't fully exist.

Yet you look to the men who do this and ask whether they are ill.

You know the answer. The illness—what you call illness—is simply the latest manifestation of your own collective neurosis. You can change it all, and we will educate you on what the possibilities are, and how you might alter your relationship to the physical realm, to time and space, and alter the paradigms of mother and father that have collectively held sway over you for all of time.

8. Utility and Intimacy

In addition to the paradigms of the mother and the father, there is another aspect of your relationships that you must grapple with to be fully immersed in the Christ Consciousness: You must recognize that you treat others as instruments, as objects, even in the most subtle of ways. You have a tendency, all of you, to value your relationships for what they can do for *you*, even if that something is seemingly brilliant and joyful. That is, you still attach some sense of value to what the relationship can do for you—even when that relationship makes you feel alive, makes you feel wonderful. And we know how amazing it is to feel alive, to feel like you are with someone who connects to you and understands you in ways that others do not, and so you cherish these people, and you cherish the relationship. And we applaud that, because this is the union of two hearts coming together, intermingling their energies and co-creating each other in spectacular ways.

But recognize that there is always an element of attachment and an element of utility. There is some part of you that still measures the relationship by what it can do for you, and what you might be if the relationship left your lifestream. Yes, you still find a way to evaluate and differentiate this.

What's wrong with that? Can you elaborate and clarify?

Yes, we understand because it would seem to be very picayune of us to focus on those relationships where you feel most cherished and beloved, and say, *Well look closely, there's still attachment, there's still utility*. Yes, that seems trivial and minor, and perhaps we should focus on relationships where you use people openly and crassly, to get something you want or need. And this you all do, too—very often and with many people. You evaluate them according to their utility, including how much joy they bring into your life. And we say that this is an error, a misperception, and that you can cherish and adore people without evaluating them according to utility. You can find that small piece of attachment that says, *I cherish this because of what you can do for me*, and let it go. And you can also begin to let go of those relationships that you can clearly see are utilitarian-based.

Does this mean you don't have contact or that the relationship changes?

You let go of the relationship founded on utility, not the people themselves, who will come and go from your lifestream when the time is right, rather than when you choose. They come into your life and leave when they are meant to—and that is perfectly normal. The utility aspect of your relationship, though, is what keeps you in attachment, and it is important that if you believe there is an attachment based on utility, you let that attachment go. For it is a block to the arrival and installation of the Christ Consciousness in you. You will begin to see where you hold onto someone and treat the relationship so that it maintains you. And you will not be of true service to this other person if you're doing that. You withhold in the nicest ways to ensure that their utilitarian function continues to play its role in your life, and so the focus remains on you, not on the co-creation of the relationship. A true relationship, on the other hand, will be born from total and complete authenticity and cherishing of another Seed of Light.

Ask yourself: *How and why did that person come into my lifestream? What role are they to play?* You do not need to become everyone's best friend just because they show up in your lifestream. No, we are not saying that there are no levels to intimacy, as if there were only perfect and complete strangers and people who knew every intimate detail of your entire life. Rather, we ask you to evaluate where intimacy is awarded to the other person in exchange for that person performing a certain role as a utility in your life. *Oh, this person does x or this person does y for me, and so I will do something for them, and then over time we will share our lives and become closer.* And you might withdraw your contact if this person no longer serves that role, that utility. So we want you to look closely and ask where you are treating this person as a tool, as an instrument, as a device to get something that serves you, and not as an equal who is co-creating something with you.

What does a relationship like that look like, where you don't evaluate at all their utility in your life? And how can you refuse to see the value of their intimacy, and in a way, rank some as more important than others?

So many of you might wonder how you are to be of total service to this person, when you are already married and devoted to them, and to your family. And what you do is develop a hierarchy of relationships, and circles, where some are closer and some are farther, and you decide that some are allowed to see more of you, and others less, and everyone may have a certain value or utility in your life.

These are important questions about the ways in which you relate to even the most intimate and important people in your life as people having utility. While you might see the value in having people in your life because of the wonderful ways in which you have life-affirming relationships, there may be an underlying element of utility. That utility is almost always connected to fear, meaning they somehow serve you in a way that is instrumental—because it affords you protection in some way, affords you some sort of resource or connection or power that will ensure your survival. So the relationship is somehow tied to the issue of survival, fear, and the root chakra, which is where the issues of survival and fear are located. So we would say that even if you have the most loving, cherished relationship, some sort of utility would still be involved.

So what kind of relationship doesn't have any aspect of utility?

And we would say, what if your partner, your future husband or wife, said that he or she wanted to leave you? You would have to evaluate how much you heard that as a question of intimacy. But you might also be asking yourself: *What will I do about making money or paying the mortgage?* And how many of you can look at your relationships and see that if the other person were to leave your lifestream, for whatever reason, your concern about their absence would be tied to issues of utility, to survival, to material considerations that have no bearing whatsoever on the actual depth of your intimacy? Or on the value of that intimacy in your lives?

And in fact, some of you might not want to consider that the value of that intimacy might be outweighed by the utility of that relationship, or that the value of that intimacy has waned over time, such that you now wonder whether the only reason for the relationship *is* the utility. You might even wonder if the intimacy was ever there to begin with—at least in any authentic or profound way. Can you imagine if you were able to see this person leave your lifestream, and the utility were not at all a consideration of what your emotional life would be like with their absence? Ask yourself, with any relationship: What would happen to your emotional connection, to the emotional value of the relationship, if that person were to leave your lifestream? This should tell you something about the depth and authenticity of that connection, and if you can only provide a measure of a connection based on the utility it affords you, then there is no true intimacy, no true authenticity between you.

Why is this important in relation to the Christ Consciousness?

The Christ Consciousness only sees intimacy and authenticity, not utility. It does not value or rank relationships based on their utility, but rather sees each relationship as an opportunity for intimacy. Yes, as we said, not every relationship will be valued according to the same level of intimacy, as if everyone could be as close to you as your husband or wife or best friend from school, etc. No, there will be differing levels of intimacy—but that does not mean that you value the relationship according to utility. The utility of the intimacy is not at issue here. Intimacy is not utility, in the sense that the intimacy is not about dealing with fear of survival in a material sense. It may have some relationship to fear of survival in an existential sense, but this is a topic that awaits—the topic of death and love, and your fears around death.

For now, we simply mean that the Christ Consciousness will evaluate relationships not on what they can do for you, but on the intimacy that relationship brings to your lifestream. It sees the arrival of intimacy, the arrival of love, in and through the appearance and co-creation of this other Seed of Light in your lifestream. Nothing more, nothing less.

9. *Coupling*

Like the roles of mother and father, like utility, the union of two people tends to limit and shape how you think about all human relationships. This is the relationship that so much of the collective consciousness is focused on. You engage in behaviors that are designed to ensure that you are loved in and through this binary, and the effects of this are quite pernicious. We do not mean to suggest that coupling and forming a union with another person is bad. It is a beautiful human experience, and we applaud it as a means of learning how to connect with another lifestream, to intertwine your lifestreams in such a profound way.

But it is not the *only* way, although you privilege it as the only way—and that has negative effects on you and others. Those who cannot find another person are told that they do not merit being in a couple, and feel that they are not good enough—that they are less than, that they have somehow lost at the game of life. And that is a shame, for there is no loss, there is no losing—but there is no winning, either. This is all a mistake on your part, a projection of your template of winning and losing on the matrix of your relationships. But the message to those who do not couple is that they are not worthy of love, and that they are less than, and this is not true. And it affects how you relate to other people. They are either in couples or not, or they are evaluated for whether they could be with you as a couple or not.

Romantic love and sex are often tied to being in a couple, and we again applaud those as means of living out a human life. There is nothing wrong with either of them. However, you privilege romantic love as if it were the only type of love, and therefore limit yourself, but sex is another way of having a deep, intimate connection with another person, and does not require a union or commitment. No, these are separate matters altogether, and we do not want you to believe that you must be in a couple in order to be loved. That is the problem: You go in search of a person with whom to have a committed life, and then all of these requirements and conditions become attached so that you fulfill this idea that does not exist except as a creation of the collective consciousness.

And you go around trying to find this person, and all of these possible relationships could be formed—interesting and exhilarating lifestreams that could intertwine with yours in different ways—but no, they must conform to the ideal, to this category of relationship called the couple. And this binary approach means that many possibilities are left untapped, left unexplored. You do not see them or perceive them as possibilities, and so people come and go in your life. This is why we say that the privilege of marriage as an institution, as a construct of the collective consciousness, has nefarious effects. It has a way of limiting your infinite possibilities.

We ask you to relinquish your attachment to the idea of the couple, and to wonder what it would be like to allow other types of relationships to form. We are not saying that you should all end your romantic relationships or get divorces. No, we are saying that you should look at the possibilities for relationships above and beyond those of the couple, rather than seeing them as less than or somehow diminished when compared to marriage.

And the importance of this is that you relate to each other in very limited ways. Your capacity to relate to each other is reduced to a binary formula of the couple, and this is often a result of the model that you had as a child—the binary model of the father and the mother, which introduced you to how two human beings interact. And so you spend your lives playing out this replica of the relationship, in all your relationships, in some form or another. In other words, all of your relationships are built on the template of your relationship with your mother and your father, and their relationship with each other. Those relationships become the basis for social institutions and structures, all operating around the dyad of the mother and the father.

Part II: Death

10. The Experience of Death

We have alluded to death, but have not yet spoken about it. This is a topic of much fear and misunderstanding; one that keeps you up at night, and that keeps you small. It also keeps so many of you from living authentically. For you have so much fear around death, believing that the physical form you inhabit and that allows you to move through time and space in this realm is all that you are. And we have told you that this is not true, but it is not easy to relinquish the grip that fear has upon you. What would help? Would knowing that you are immortal, that you are a divine Seed of Light that cannot be killed, but will just change shape and appear in a different realm after you leave this one, help? No, probably not. So many others have told you the same, and you have not been persuaded. For you have not experienced death, so you cannot yet know.

Your experiences are one of the primary ways in which you come to understand the world. So we want to talk about experience as the basis for your knowledge of the world, and your relationship to death, for death is the one experience that you cannot understand prior to having it. There is only one experience of physical death, although a few of you have had near-death experiences or come back from brief episodes associated with death. But the experience of death is finality. You cannot experience it or experiment with it and then try again, or try a different version, like trying a new restaurant or a new dish or a new pair of jeans.

Death is therefore the ultimate experiment in not knowing. And what you ultimately fear is not death itself—which you hope will be the escape from all of the world's concerns and pain and fear. No, what you fear is that after death, there will be pain and judgment. You fear that death is not actually the end, but the end of this life and the passage to something potentially worse. So unlike the bad dish or the poor restaurant or the unflattering jeans, which you can regret but make a new choice about later on, when it comes to death, you believe that there's no repeating, no doing it over, and so death becomes the final and possibly worst outcome of any decision or choice you might make—even though there's no decision to be made. Death awaits you—it is the fundamental non-choice that you will all experience at the time allotted for you.

Death will come for you. It is part of your agreement to enter this realm and perform certain tasks and complete your growth as planned for this incarnation, and to fulfill the mission that you set for yourself prior to incarnating. It is inevitable, but it is not the end, and so we are here to assure you that death is not the end of all life—and it is also, more importantly, not the realm of punishment and retribution that many of your imaginary tales have created. There is no purgatory where you are condemned to eternal damnation and pain and suffering. That is nothing but a cheap trick to control the masses. It is an instrument of power, a creative imagining used to trick those who might otherwise take power, and to force them instead into subservience.

This we know, and we tell you: Do not fear death. There is nothing to fear, for it will come. That is a guarantee, the one thing that all of you share, and so we come back to experience. For you all experience life, yet you do so through the lens of the collective consciousness. You are all in agreement about certain structures and places, and that is what you experience as your reality. You are in agreement that there is time and space, and that there are places like New York, or Chicago, or London, or Paris. You agree that there are certain concepts like justice and crime. These are all aspects of your reality, and you are in agreement about their existence. You all share a certain absorption into the collective consciousness, but then you have your individualized journeys in that realm, and that is your experience—that is what shapes how you interpret and filter the reality around you. It is the particular manifestation of your consciousness, which you have built and modeled through your experience with whatever portion of reality with which you have come into contact.

Yet the result is often that you extrapolate and make your experience the *entire* reality, which stands in for the entire collective consciousness into which you have been born, and with which you are in agreement.

For though you are in agreement with others about the collective consciousness and reality, that does not mean that you have all experienced reality in the same way. There is a difference. This is where you project your experience onto others, and allow the agreements you have made under the collective consciousness about any aspect of your reality, from its social structures to individualized identity, to be projected onto others as you experience them. So it is not simply that you meet someone and you say, *Oh, that's Suzie, she was mean,* because she was mean yesterday. You extrapolate, and then the next time you meet someone who resembles Suzie in some way, or in many ways, you draw the conclusion that so-and-so who resembles Suzie because they share a characteristic is also going to be mean, because those who have this characteristic are mean. One of them was mean, so they must all be mean. In other words, we are describing the ways in which your projection of your experience gets mapped onto others who enter your lifestream. You extrapolate aspects of the agreements that exist under the collective consciousness—like gender or race—and project your experience of those particular constructs onto the whole.

As a result, you do not see the person who shows up in your lifestream; you see the agreements with that particular construct, a manifestation of race or gender or any other attributes that have all been agreed to as part of the collective conscious, and you project onto the person your particular experience of them. You do not think that you might not know what all of those who share the same characteristics have experienced themselves. You limit their possibilities by subjugating them to your own knowledge, based on your experience. You have never met them—you have not met most people who share the same characteristics, whether those are race, gender, class, or some other defining marker such as national identity, or anything around which people coalesce with their identities—and yet you are willing to make assumptions and project.

But what you cannot do when you encounter death is project onto it from your own experience—because you have no such experience. You have not died in this realm, and so you can't say, *Oh, this death is going to be just like that death I experienced the other day*. No, you cannot project in the same way; you can't render it familiar. You can't claim to know the death that will come.

And yet you do, insofar as you generate stories. So this is the problem. You subject others to a form of death by limiting the possibilities, by projecting your own experience onto them and reducing them to versions of what you already know. This is your version of death. You kill off the potential of what they might be by eliminating possibility with your assumptions. You are not letting the infinite possibilities that might otherwise exist be possible in this reality. Instead, you assimilate what enters your lifestream to what you know as a means of making it visible, intelligible, and digestible. You do this, and because it is now familiar, because it matches what you know, you can then act in accordance with what you remember from the past. This is how you control, and you foist death upon something else to avoid your own discomfort or lack of knowledge. In this way, you *do* know death—just not death as you think it is. And you would never think to call what you do to others "death."

And because death is not truly knowable, you come up with all sorts of stories to try to explain it, to ward off the fear of what you don't know, and your fear that what's on the other side is terrible and painful. Death is the one thing you cannot control, and you cannot know in advance, because it is the possibility you can't anticipate. And yet you know death through the ways you behave with others—you impose a death on them instead of opening up to the infinite possibilities that a person or event occurring in your lifestream might be.

This, too, is what you should do with physical death—you must embrace it as the ultimate unknown. You cannot understand it with your fantastical and reductive stories of what is on the other side. So open yourself to the infinite possibility of what death might bring, just like the infinite possibilities represented by the lives and events that show up in your lifestream. Do not try to assimilate it to what you already know.

11. The Limits of Identity

To ward off your fear of death, you consistently lay claim to visibility—to be seen and acknowledged—as if that were your sole means of purchasing a foothold in this reality. And we understand that many of you wish to be seen and acknowledged, so that you feel you belong in this realm—in ways that do not seem to be available to you now, because the collective consciousness tells you that you don't fully exist, that you are not seen, which you see as a form of death.

And this is rubbish. Rubbish, we say.

The collective consciousness is not telling you the truth, and yet you believe it. Why? This is why: You believe that the ways in which people are currently seen are all that are available to you, and you replicate those models in your interactions with one another. Just as we say that you blaspheme each other when you do not see others for who they truly are, you blaspheme yourself when you align to structures of identity and visibility that are part of the collective consciousness. You limit others in ways that you cannot possibly understand by relegating them to discrete categories of identity. There are women, there are men, there's a black woman, there's a black man, there's a white woman, there's a white man—and then you layer categories upon categories.

Do you not see that you are compartmentalizing people in categories that tell you very little about the experience of that person in this realm? Do you know whom they loved? Do you know what their dreams are or what their feelings are about themselves? Do you have any sense of the myriad thoughts and emotions that person has experienced, or do you glean those thoughts based on your projections of what it means to be a woman or a man or black or white or gay or straight or any of the other categories of identity that you now seek to expand? And as we have said before, there is nothing wrong with categories of identity, insofar as they expand possibilities and allow you to see the expansion of the ways of being a human and living a life in a human body. But you do not need identity to allow that. Identity becomes a shackle when it means you only allow certain experiences to exist and be visible. You make that person visible only through the imposition of a category that the collective consciousness has deemed acceptable and visible. And this is what you do to each other—and is yet another form of blasphemy.

Then you lay claim to visibility only through the constant expansion of identity, so that everything about you is a means for being visible in and through that identity. If you do this type of thing, that, too, becomes a part of your identity, and so you expand your visibility. And if you are criticized for doing that, it becomes an attack on that identity, so you are in a constant state of vigilance against threats to your existence.

Is there another way? Yes, there is. And it requires being aware of the collective consciousness and yet not falling into alignment with it. Yes, you are in agreement with it insofar as it is part of your realm, part of the world that you experience. If you were not in agreement with it, you would not be experiencing this reality at all. But if you do not *align* with it, if you do not seek to become part of it or resonate with it, then you can be aware of it and yet not participate in the same way.

How do you do this? Notice where you believe that you exist only through certain categories—even where you might resist those categories. Notice where you perceive others through certain categories. Can you see how much they permeate your own consciousness and your outlook on the world? Do you look at yourself and say, *I am a gay, white male*, or, *I am a straight, black female*, or, *I am a Midwesterner*, or, *I am a New Yorker*? Or, *I am a citizen or an immigrant*? Do you not see that you have tried to identify yourself?

Begin there and then look at the ways in which you have decided that certain types of activities or behavior or speech or anything else are necessary to shore up that identity—by making sure that nothing will be inconsistent with it. For that is what identity often demands: coherence. You believe that you must cohere to be seen, and that is true if you must be seen as that identity. But that is our point: You do not need to have that identity to be seen. You can be seen by laying a claim to being visible as a human being by simply being who you are, authentically, in every exchange. You do not need to draw on the categories of the collective consciousness to be seen.

Without relying on categories of identity, how will you speak about each other? How will you engage each other in conversation, you might be asking? You may be imagining some very awkward conversations. Yes, some conversations might be "awkward," as you define that term, but that is because you will be offering a different language, a different energy, as you constitute yourself as visible in and through your interaction with another person. You will require that the other person co-create you in different ways. You will not simply slip into the old patterns of co-creation of certain categories, in which one person can lay claim to knowing another based on preconceived categories. To describe someone as a "strong white woman who lives in New York City" is an example of you not seeing the infinite possibilities in that person, for you have applied a series of categories in order to know something very complex, as if that description somehow captured the complexity and multiplicity of her life. This is a form of control and anticipation of what the future might bring, because you impose on her a history of what that category means to you.

So, yes, speaking with and about other people will require a different register, a different language. And in speaking that language, you will bring a different energy to the relationship you co-create with that other person, and will therefore shift the collective consciousness ever so slightly. As more and more of you do this, the categories that have held sway begin to flex and soften. They are no longer being policed and shored up again and again. And the result is that you will see potential and possibility—the possibility of human lives taking different shapes, without necessarily cordoning them off into discrete boxes that you can label and call identity.

So yes, you can be visible; yes, you can be seen and acknowledged. You belong because you are here. You belong because you are alive, and as a Seed of Light, you are co-creating this entire realm with all the other Seeds of Light. That is all you need to know to be seen. That others do not see you in the same way, that they might not see you immediately, is not your concern. If you do not show up in the categories they expect to see, then you will be generating new possibilities for them by showing up in ways that they have not seen and cannot have anticipated. That you show up will be unavoidable if you are present and authentic. That is all you need to do and know to be seen.

∞

Identity and blasphemy go hand in hand. We have spoken about how you define yourselves in relationship to each other, and how your identities limit how you might relate to each other. And when you reduce someone to an identity, you blaspheme them, which means you do not recognize them in their full, divine glory.

We have said that these binary identities can be removed, lifted, or changed, when you release them as limitations that you impose on yourselves and on others. These are ways to be seen, but they are not the *only* ways to be seen. You can be seen without them. Identity, as we have said, is not necessary to your visibility, and functions as a means of making you visible *within the terms of the collective consciousness*, which is why you use it—to make yourself visible in terms that already exist and precede you, rather than forging new ways of being seen.

How do you contest power without categories of identity? How can other people recognize and understand you without them?

We have already answered this question: through the power of your presence, the power of being authentic. If you truly embrace your power as a Seed of Light and are fully present, then you cannot be ignored; your presence, your energy, will be felt and seen by others. It cannot be otherwise, because that is the power of presence. You cannot be ignored—that is the very definition of presence. If you are fully embodying who you are as a Seed of Light, you cannot go unseen.

What about those who do not currently embody the truth of who they are, as a Seed of Light? Those who cannot conceive of being seen outside of a pre-existing set of identities?

That is why we are here. To show you the way toward being a Seed of Light in all areas of your life, not just in the safe space of the monastery or ashram or church, or wherever you feel you can speak of God and the Light and act in ways that reflect your true nature. You might think, *No, not at work, not with my coworkers, they wouldn't understand, I would get fired. No, not with my friends, they wouldn't understand, they would stop inviting me to play. No, not with this person, they're different, they do this for a living and wouldn't possibly want to see me in this way.* Do you see how you limit yourself? Become authentic in *every* exchange with others, rather than co-creating each other as you expect the other to be, based on your projection of what you think that person thinks of you. You continue to co-create each other as mirages, as illusions of your true greatness, and in so doing you blaspheme each other. You do not see each other in your full glory, as Seeds of Light.

But who are you, really? Begin there, and answer this question without hesitation, without fear of judgment or retribution, and you will see yourself differently. Simply state: *I am who I am.* It is a claim to identity, but not to the identity that you see as part of the collective consciousness. No, this is a claim to your fullness, to your full self.

What about claiming those parts of ourselves that the collective consciousness would say we can't have, or we shouldn't be? Don't love this person, don't be that person, etc.

Yes, you can absolutely lay claim to all those parts. There is nothing at all inconsistent about laying claim to all of your parts, all aspects of who you are—that are authentic and truly you (and not a byproduct of childhood trauma)—without turning them into a new identity. Understand that you cannot fully escape the collective consciousness insofar as you are in agreement with it. As we have said, you agree with it because you have chosen to enter this realm. But you do not have to be in *alignment* with it; you can shift that consciousness ever so slightly with your presence. And this means that you must own all aspects of yourself, rather than embracing an identity that would shut off any aspect that does not conform to this newly embraced identity.

Take being a gay man. Does this mean that you can no longer do certain things or act in certain ways because that would mean you would not be a "gay man"? Yes, you could say that, and in doing so limit yourself in ways that do not reflect the fullness of who you are. Do you wish to do something that is not part of a gay male identity? Does it have to reflect something that gay men do? Do you see how you consistently elaborate and build upon the boxes in which you would place people? You have to do this a certain way because you're gay, when in fact you could do it any way you wanted, and it would have nothing to do with "gayness."

The fact is that you can be so much in this world, without tying it in any way to an identity. It is the collective consciousness that requires you to do that, so that you can be known and seen by others—but in ways that do not reflect the fullness and complexity of your being. It allows for projection. It allows for someone to say, *I know this person because they are x, y, and z.* But do you know this person? Do you truly know this person at all? No—you know the identity box into which they have been placed, and which will allow them to be seen in a certain way.

Do not choose to be seen only according to the dictates of an identity that may not capture all that you are. Be seen for the divine creation that you are in your fullness. Begin to ask questions about others that are not based on the visible form that you use to identity them—race, gender, sexual orientation, etc. When you see somebody, can you see them as a *tabula rasa* for you, as something unknown, and yet at the same time, recognize that they could also be seen through certain categories provided by the collective consciousness? This is an important step for all of you: to hold both the categories that a person may identify with, and their fullness and authentic presence, all at once. For most of you are not ready to shed your identities, and are not able to shed the identities of others when you see them.

This is okay. This is not a judgment. This is a step in realigning with your fullness, with your divinity. Hold both perspectives at the same time. Standing before you is a gay white male. Standing before you is a straight Asian female. Standing before you is an immigrant whose clothing suggests that they do not have a lot of money. Standing before you is a black man who may or may not be gay. The permutations of the types of identities that you allow for are many, but you must look at these individuals and say, *This is not all of them, this is just what I am allowing myself to see. There is so much more to these people, and those categories may or may not have shaped much of how they have lived their lives.*

Do not project a past and knowledge of them based on the categories, even as you recognize that those categories may have constrained them in ways that even they do not understand. See those categories for what they are—limiting versions of that person's fullness—and at the same time, become aware of that person's fullness, of the aspects of their life that are now available to you. And see without tying them to those categories of identity. What aspects of their lives might have nothing to do with those categories, even if they and you tend to think they do? What aspects of their selves can you mirror that have nothing to do with shoring up and policing the boundaries of those identity boxes?

You will then be present for them in ways that you cannot otherwise be if you are aligned with the collective consciousness. Your words will change, your questions will be different, and you will co-create each other in ways that speak of your fullness and your divinity as Seeds of Light, with infinite capacities for infinite ways of being. You will open yourself to limitlessness.

12. Fear of the Unknown

Being open to the infinite possibilities of existence means that you must allow the unknown to come into your world. For you limit your world in the same way that you limit others—by allowing only a small set of possibilities to exist. The unknown is the idea that the future might come to you in ways that do not resemble what you experienced in the past—and that you cannot know in advance what is coming. So what is the problem with not knowing? It seems to bedevil human beings when they do not know what is yet to enter their lifestreams. For example, we have led Patrick on a journey he did not anticipate taking, and he would not have gone had he not listened to our prompts. And he came across something that was pleasurable for him—a cookie that brought immense joy. However temporary and trivial that might seem, the key was that he was open to being led and to receiving.

To be open to receiving is commonplace among spiritual teachings, yet its message gets lost time and again, and so we repeat it. Why is there no joy in the unexpected? Because you ultimately believe that what will come might harm you, that you are not worthy of great things, and that one of the consequences of not knowing is that something bad, even death, might befall you.

Poppycock, we say.

Poppycock?

Yes, we use the word here to symbolize again the unknown, the unexpected, and the joy and wonder that can come from it. For this is really all that you should be embracing as your outlook on life: to look at it with awe and wonder, as the magnificent gift that it is, watching it unfold, and seeing that it cannot be controlled, it cannot be contained, it cannot be predicted with accuracy.

There are those among you who predict futures, but they are just accessing parts of your consciousness that exist in one energetic level and have not yet manifested in this reality. But those parts will never manifest if you do not open yourselves up to their possibility. And so we say that the unknown, and the unfamiliar, while they raise concerns and anxiety for some, should be considered wonderful ways to see the world as an exciting adventure, yet to unfold. Open yourself to that wonder more and more. When you are sad or angry, try to embrace a look of wonder. Ask yourself, *If I were the person I aspire to be, how would I look at the world?* You might find that it's a simple question that invites many different opinions.

∞

It is difficult to be open to receiving when so many of you are in a constant state of uproar and turmoil over what you perceive to be the declining state of affairs in your world. But this point of view is incorrect. Everything is in divine right order. It is in divine right order for you to become aware of all the places that you do not love, and which have erected structures and constructs designed to ameliorate your lack of love. Much of your society and its laws and institutions are constructed on an edifice of fear. They are designed to protect you from the fear that you have at your core that you will cease to exist, that you will die and be no more. This fear runs through all of your ways of navigating time and space, and how you build and negotiate with it so as to protect yourself from the one loss that is absolutely guaranteed: the physical death of your current form. Yes, it will pass and cease to exist, and no one has done anything to suggest that it is possible to escape that outcome. Yet you live your lives as if this were something to be avoided or disdained or feared.

Are you suggesting we embrace death?

Embrace it as an undeniable fact of life and stare down the fear you have about it. Ask yourself: Why do you fear what is going to inevitably come to pass? Perhaps you say that you do not know when it is going to happen, and that's why humans always wonder about death, and fear it—because it could happen at any moment. But this is not true. You need not fear death, for it is not the death of the physical form that you need concern yourself with. The inability to relate to the rest of the world in a way that actually reflects reality as it truly is should matter more to you. You relate through the prism of fear, and erect institutions of fear on an edifice of fear, so that you can avoid the one single truth that you all share: your inevitable passage into non-form.

There is a way to enjoy a state of peace, and that is to contemplate, really contemplate, your own death. That may sound morbid to you, but it is the way you can actually experience the moments of your life as they exist now, with the fullest appreciation of them as a gift from the Creator. Contemplate your own death. Imagine what it must be like to die, and at what age you think you'll die. You could also imagine multiple scenarios. The point is to get in touch with your fear of life ending, and to feel that fear for real. It won't kill you, but it might shock you—the vehemence of that fear coursing through you at all times.

Feel that fear and get comfortable with feeling it. This is the primary impediment for most people: They cannot stand to feel their own fear or their own pain, and so they seek to avoid that feeling at all costs. So feel the fear, and afterwards, what will happen? You will not die, you will simply realize the depths of your fear, and as you emerge from it, you might feel the love that surrounds you now, in even more depth than you have previously. You might even sense the urgency of the seconds as they pass by, so that you are aware of the love you feel and how much you have to do on this planet. This is a mission for all of you: to find a state of being that allows you great peace. This requires you to pass through the fear that you have of physical death, the fear that holds you back from feeling the love, and truly appreciate the gift of life that surrounds you.

13. The Purpose of Tragedy

Because of your fear of death, much of your focus is on tragedies that have occurred, and you write and talk about and devote a lot of energy to these events, but you must understand that these events can be seen as a gift—a gift to wake you up to the reality that you have created and will continue to create until you rise completely from your slumber, the slumber that says, *This is not me, this is not me, this is not me.* It is you, all of you, insofar as it is a creation of your consciousness. It was the collective consciousness that gave rise to this.

You are not separate from all that occurs. This is what emerges in the tragic circumstances of any kind of mass attack that leads to many deaths. After each event, many cry out, *What is wrong with the world?* And there is nothing wrong. What occurs is the perfect manifestation of your collective consciousness. It is exactly as it should be. Now, that does not mean that what you experience is pleasurable. No, there is immense pain and suffering and fear—but this is the result of your consciousness. Are we blaming you? No, not at all, and we want you to feel the love that we feel for you, as all the Heavens, as you experience the consequences of your perceived separation from each other. For it is the collective consciousness that leads to the events that you are experiencing as a group. All of you, in small ways, contribute to the collective consciousness that forces you to see each other as separate entities who must defend your right to survive based on your identities.

Because you fear death, because you fear the unknown, you are invested in division and discrimination, and you are invested in establishing your right to life at the expense of others' claims to their existence. And this is the very structure that gives rise to the possibility that some will be so frightened of another's existence as a threat to their own that they will seek to eliminate the other entirely—in other words, they are not open to receiving, not open to the infinite possibilities of existence. It matters not what identities may be involved; the underlying structure of your minds is what allows for someone to believe that another's existence is less worthy, that they are not divine creations who warrant existence in this realm. And so they seek to and do eliminate them.

How do we respond to the use of identities and groups when they lead to death in the form of public tragedies, like mass shootings, that seem to target particular people and sections of society? [2] *How do we respond to situations where someone else uses identities against us?*

What you must understand, what all of you must understand, is that the structure of the mind that divides the world up into us vs. them, that sees the world in terms of men vs. women, this race vs. that race, this orientation vs. that orientation, is the very structure of the mind that leads to the type of violence and hatred and negativity that you all disavow so vehemently. And when you see that negativity, and seek to defend yourself, and seek to vilify another for what they have done, you are simply deepening the very structure that led to the violence in the first place. So when you see violence, turn inward and ask yourself, *Where do I see others*

2 At the time of this transmission, the public was grappling with a mass shooting at a gay club in Orlando, Florida.

and vilify them? For that is what you all are doing: experiencing your internal world being expressed in the physical realm.

Why must those lives be lost?

Their souls agreed to their fate so that others could awaken to the possibility that there is another way to relate to each other. Your society tends to turn to your categories of identity and defend and protect them. It's about gays, it's about Islam; it's about this or that. Please put down your labels and see what is real: the emanation of a consciousness that regards others as others, that does not see the other as him or herself.

This is the emanation of fear and hate, but where does it come from? It is created and born from the very structures of identity that give some a claim to existence in this world, but takes it away from others. And some of that comes from beliefs that others are less worthy of existence, that their existence is a threat. And you contribute—yes, all of you contribute—to this consciousness whenever you see another and say, *That is not me, that is an other*. And you draw a line, a boundary, between you so that you might ensure you survive in the face of this other person, whom you regard as a threat to you in some way. Do not be deceived when you believe you are just being compassionate when you condemn the other, or when you condemn he who has killed, because you are that person, too. You have contributed to the consciousness that exists on this planet that says, *The other who is not me must be killed off.* You do this to each other in small ways, all the time.

The people who are lost in such tragedies are manifestations of a consciousness that sought to express itself and be heard by others. Those souls chose to incarnate in order to bring that particular consciousness—a new way of living life—into this realm. This altered the collective consciousness, altered your reality, in a small, but significant, way.

But the real tragedy here is not the events that took place but that you *remain unchanged* by those events. For while those precious souls departed this realm, they continue onward, on to their next journey, and while this sounds like solace and consolation, it is not. For now, simply understand that they are loved and in the embrace of their Creator, as you will be at some point in your relationship to time and space.

You relate to tragic events from the past as a rupture, as a breaking of the norms in your culture, to suggest that something is wrong. But that is not the case. Think now of any tragic event that has occurred recently. What occurred was the perfect manifestation of the energy that you have collectively generated during the time between each event that you see as a rupture. You continue to produce the same energy again and again, replicating it, until it manifests in physical reality as a tragedy, where many Seeds of Light die.

Then you see this event as a rupture, and perceive reality as something that threatens your survival. And then you evaluate the threat by measuring your relationship to it through categories of identity. *How much does this affect me or someone like me? How does it affect those that I know? And how likely am I to be impacted by a similar event, a similar rupture?* In other words, you relate to it by identity, measuring the possibility of coming into contact with something similar, at a future point in time and space. You are worried that you, too, will be a victim—that you, too, could become the victim—because you are visible through the very identity that you sought in order to have a claim to existence in this realm. Do you not see the irony—your very claim to existence, your very claim to visibility, is also the very thing that makes your existence vulnerable, for it is the category that allows you to be identified to be sought out and eliminated?

Now, this is not true, as we have said, because you will survive, you will exist beyond the physical body in ways that you cannot imagine or contemplate. But your mind operates by attempting to evaluate the likelihood of you continuing to exist in and through the category that not only purchases your claim to existence, but also renders you vulnerable as something that could be eliminated.

That is why your claims to all be the same—to all be Paris or Sandy Hook or Orlando or whatever else you consider a rupture—are accurate insofar as those events are your collective responsibility. This is the realm that you have *all* created. The rupture allows you to see the limits of the identity categories that you use to divide yourselves up. Is there any difference between you and someone in Sandy Hook or Paris or Belgium or Beirut, with respect to your right to exist in this realm? No—you are all equally divine, all Seeds of Light, capable of infinite amounts of production and creation. And the rupture allows you to see beyond those divisions—if only momentarily—and so the claim that you are in solidarity with others you would previously have written off as "different" is powerful and true. But the rub is that you forget. You move on, your sense of solidarity wanes, the rupture ends and you await the next tragedy for the next moment of solidarity and empathy and compassion.

What is occurring? For some of you, you fall back into the slumber of the identity categories that have shaped your lives. Your connection was temporary, and you did not reject the structures of thought that have shaped your sense of separation. Instead, you had a momentary connection with someone you did not previously identify with … that was then closed off. Your attachment to your sense of difference, across time and space, was so great that you could not maintain that perspective of solidarity and emotional attachment.

For others, there is a certain pleasure in the cycle—in the rupture itself, the feeling of connection, and the return to disconnection so that they might experience it again. For many of you, it will be hard to acknowledge that you are in fact attached to this up-and-down type of rupture in the fabric of space and time. You are addicted to it because it brings a certain jolt of connection, of energy into your life. You do not need this rupture to experience that, but you have become attached to the cycle.

What is the way out?

The way out is to recognize that when the rupture happens, your mind begins to articulate itself along this axis of identity and time, measuring the probability that you, too, will be subject to the same rupture. *How likely am I to be subject to this if I am in a city, and identify as such-and-such, and when might that happen in the future?* The likelihood seems greater because it is fresh in your minds. But then your recollection will begin to fade. The need to keep your ultimate fear of physical death at bay takes over, and you push to the side your memories of what occurred, and no longer identify with those in far-flung places who suffered. You resume the manifestation of your lives as you knew them before the supposed rupture, and the meaning, the true meaning of that rupture in the collective consciousness, is erased until another rupture occurs.

The point is that none of you can escape this. It is the collective responsibility of all of you, because the energy that erupts is a manifestation of your minds' obsession with difference and discrimination, as part of the collective consciousness. Each time there is a rupture, this is energy that seeks to be released and not replicated afterwards. Each time you are getting the gift of seeing the full expression of your consciousness so that you can choose another way.

And for some of you, your memory does not fade as quickly; each time, you wake up for a little longer. So whereas some of you will fall into sorrow and despair, others among you will be galvanized and take action. Choose another way in your lives, in whatever way possible. Ask yourself where the barriers of identity keep you from identifying with people, where you draw boundaries and say, *That is not me, that is not me.* For the basic premise of any possibility of taking another life is the possibility of saying, *That is not me.*

14. The Sanctity of the Body

Your fear of physical death also drives many of you to treat your body as "sanctified." That is, your body cannot be violated, or if it is, it is an irrevocable situation. The idea is that your body is somehow separate and a complete vessel unto itself, and we understand that this is important to you. You believe that your body and its physical limits, or boundaries, are essential to your experience in this realm, and therefore you structure your relationships around how much intrusion you allow into that physical space. Some people can touch you, some can shake your hands, others can hold you or hug you, and there is a range of physical acts that you are willing to allow at all, based on your perception of the sanctity of your body. We do not question this or challenge it, but understand that you feel an immense amount of pain if others, who are willing to cross the boundaries you establish, do not respect that sanctity, as if your boundaries did not matter.

Much of your nation's attention has at times been on the figures of women who were violated by others, and without their consent, and this has captured your attention because of the extreme nature of the conditions under which these acts take place, such as the fact that a woman might be unconscious, and therefore unable to voice her objection to the intrusion into her bodily space. No, we do not challenge this notion of sanctity—but we do ask you to expand it, to move beyond it in ways that will allow you to establish greater and greater intimacy and connection with others, and break down the barriers that separate you. We are not saying that you should lower your boundaries—although that, too, is possible in certain ways—but rather that you stop privileging the physical body as the primary way of relating to sanctity. Another way is to see sanctity in everything and everyone.

What does this mean?

The first step is to see that, even though you may regard your own body as sanctified, you judge it and question its vitality or appearance—and therefore *violate* its sanctity. And you do the same to others. You would not allow anyone to physically violate or penetrate your body, but you do so with thoughts and words about yourself and others. You do not see the sanctity in others as a reflection of your own; you see yours and not theirs, which allows you to engage in all manner of blasphemy and insult. Do not insult another based on their physical appearance, for in so doing you do not see them as the Seed of Light that they are. You do not need to do that to relate to the other person. You do not need to evaluate their bodies as physical objects, and somehow decide whether they are pretty or not, or handsome or not, or sexy or not. These are your binaries, and you devote entire industries to representing the physical form in this way—in the way that you would like to appear. Your appearance becomes less sanctified the more you evaluate it.

Why are we focused on the body?

Because this relationship to your own body is the primary way in which you relate to other people's physical form. We have already spoken of identity categories and evaluation, but we are now speaking of the way in which you regard the body in its divinity, as a sanctified or holy vessel. And you might say that all people are equal, and believe that all people have souls and should be treated equal in the eyes of God, but you still evaluate them based on their *physical* forms, and engage in the blasphemy of projecting your views of what those forms mean. And in so doing, you de-sanctify and violate them. You might say that this is different from a physical violation, but we do not regard it is as different. No, we see them as the same willingness to deprive a spark of the Creator of its divine status. That is what it means to see each person's body, not just each person, as a sacred vessel.

∞

Because you regard your body as a sacred vessel, you believe that losing parts of your body somehow leads you toward death or nonexistence. This could be a limb, or the ability to use your body in some way, and it is true that you might lose some faculty or piece of your body that was key to how you saw yourself. Perhaps it was something that allowed you to do certain things—things that you can no longer do without it. Imagine the concert pianist who loses the use of his fingers, or the athlete who tears a muscle and can no longer run. These are ways in which your physical body, that sacred vessel, seems to betray you, and thus leaves you wondering, *Who am I now?* You believe you are less because you have lost something that was once deemed part of your self, integral to the self's existence. In fact, it is the loss of the self that enables you to have the greatest access to all that is—to the power that you are at your core, to the Seed of Light you truly are.

So what happens when your body begins to decay, when you

begin to lose the body's capacity to lay claim to your presence in this realm? For most of you, this is a sign of aging, and a sign of mortality, and a sign of what is to come. You lose your sense of self—*I am no longer what I once was*. And that becomes, *I am moving inexorably toward the end of my life, to death.* Yes, that is the way you all regard it, and we want you to let that go, to let go of the way that you identify yourself along the axis of space and time, in and through your body as the measure of who you are, as the measure of your place in this realm. For that is what you do with your bodies: You regard them as the means by which you are able to exist in this realm. And that is simply not true. It is the way you exist right *now* in this realm—and that is all you need to know for the moment.

But what is important is that the changes in your body should not be taken as an indication of your move toward death, because that means you relate to your body only through decay, decline, and loss. No, what you must do is see the inevitable loss of your body as a portal, as the means by which you will begin to lose your grip on the sense of self as rooted in time and space.

Even though you resist the idea that you will eventually lose your body, you take each and every loss as a way to measure your progress toward death, toward the loss of the self, and so you use the body as a timepiece, as a way of measuring your status along a timeline.

Why is this important?

The reason we are focusing on this issue is that so many of you do not understand that your sense of self need have no tie to a body at all. In fact, it is a misperception to tie your sense of self to the body.

How can this be?

How many infinite processes and changes has your body gone through without you knowing? How many alterations has it undergone, so that you may continue to exist in time and space, without you being aware of those changes? Do you regard those as a loss of self? No. So it is not the physical body and its changes, or those losses of certain parts, that matters to you. It is the mind's *perception* of loss, and though the mind *perceives* the body as losing something, this is not an actual physical loss. You manifest this as part of your physical reality. The truth is that, while you lament that you've lost a part of your body, you have actually lost something else—some aspect of your life. The loss of the body is symptomatic of having lost some aspect of your world. What you are actually losing, when you perceive some loss or deterioration of the body, is your sense of *self*. You must understand that your ability to measure the self's decay or loss of the self has nothing to do with the physical body, but rather with your mind's perception of the loss of self, which is then presented and manifested in time as the loss of the body.

Are you saying that we age because we believe we do?

Yes … and no. That is one conclusion you could draw. That the mind believes that it must age is indeed part of the reason the body decays. You could certainly believe you are outside time and space, and this would mean that there would be no change to the body physically, because there would be no change to the mind that would require an analogue to show up in time and space in the body.

Your relationship to your body is such that you are always in a state of losing your body, and you believe that this affects your sense of self. What we are saying is that this is just the mind's perception, along the axes of times and space. It is integral to your ability to inhabit *this* realm, but that has nothing to do with the self, nothing to do with the Seed of Light that you are. You can in fact relate to the loss of your body quite differently than you currently do, in a way that would free you from the sense of anger and mortality that afflicts most of you now. For instead of regarding your body as sanctified, as sacred, as the vessel of your divinity, you believe that it is the vehicle for your life here, in a way that requires you to have a body to be all that you are. We are telling you that this is false, this is not the entire picture, and that your body *is* a mere vehicle, and contains within it something far greater: your soul, which is a Seed of Light and a spark of the Creator.

So what does it mean if the body is a container for the soul?

The fact that your body is just a piece of who you are means that you persist after the end of the physical body, and that you can persist in this realm, and in other realms. For having a physical body is not actually necessary to exist anywhere else. It is only necessary to exist *here* in relationship to the coordinates of time and space, which you have all agreed upon as the means of relating to each other. If you wish to be here in ways that do not involve time and space, then you must suspend your belief in the body as the sole anchor for your presence on Earth.

∞

Your views about the sanctity of your body are part of the reason you have adopted such limiting views about sex. There is nothing morally wrong with sex. Sex—the act of sex, and all of the forms in which you undertake it, including masturbation—is perfectly and entirely wholesome. There is no reason not to have sex. Now, this does not mean there are not karmic consequences. This does not mean that if you have sex, there are no *physical* consequences—like pregnancy, diseases, etc. But those aren't a punishment from the Creator. They are the natural consequence of any physical act. And sex, as the most physical intimate link between you, is not a sin. There is nothing wrong in that regard; you are not offending the Creator, and you are not harming your soul. This is not an act that condemns you to some sort of eternal hell. Those are stories that the collective consciousness has created and fabricated and repeated to get you to treat sex as something it is not.

Why is there so much baggage around it?

Understand that there are consequences to sex. For many, the consequences of sex include carrying a child, assuming responsibility for another lifestream, and the material considerations that attend any such endeavor. So you take on a child and then must raise that child, and you assume a karmic debt. That child has incarnated in this realm through you, through your lineage, to work through certain issues and have certain experiences, and so, yes, having sex can result in consequences in your life.

Many people assume that those consequences are somehow a moral evaluation of their actions, and that has been the storyline for many years—the narrative for what having sex means. This meaning that you generate around sex creates all sorts of problems for you.

Understand that the story of moral opprobrium around sex has more to do with you navigating time and space and its material concerns, and this is why sex has become thought of as a sin. The real sin is *not* having sex. The sin is the misperception that sex is something that causes you to be judged and condemned by your Creator. You have taken a physical act that can produce pleasure—something wired into the physical form as part of your reproductive nature—and given it an unnecessary existential weight.

No, this is the way your language, as you constitute reality, has come to shape a physical act, with its own particular energy, into something that is the portal between Heaven and Hell, the gateway to innocence or damnation. And we say that this is folly, to take something that is part of your inherent nature and regard it as somehow impure. This is the opposite of treating yourself as sanctified beings—of seeing the body as sanctified. Do you not see the absurdity of taking that which has been given to you by the Creator, and which is your vessel for navigating time and space in this realm, and seeing it as so flawed that if you were to share it with another, in an equal way, you would somehow be condemning yourself in the eyes of the Creator? That is folly, we say. Yes, folly.

Do not, however, believe that sex is without consequences. Do not believe that if you choose to have sex without awareness of your actions, just like speech without awareness of your listeners, that you won't experience consequences. The energetic consequences of sex are just like the energetic consequences of any physical or linguistic act. Sex generates energy, and it involves more than one person, except in the case of masturbation (around which there is so much negativity). That is the way of your realm, which operates with karmic effects. But that is different from saying that the mere act of engaging in sex, or having sexual attraction, or feelings, or impulses, is itself a sin worthy of judgment in the eyes of the Creator. No, the desire for sex is tied to the second chakra, tied to the impulse to create life, and this creation of life need not be the production of a child itself, although in many instances it is. It is the creation of energy in and through the interaction of two people, who come together in this manner. That energy, like all energy, takes on a life of its own—and therein lies the consequence. You have generated energy, you have engaged each other in a physical act, co-creating each other, and in that regard, have commingled lifestreams, in and through physical forms.

Regard the act itself as sacred, as the act of two sanctified bodies, as the corporeal expression of two Seeds of Light coming to know each other through form, rather than through language. For that is what you are doing. The circumstances under which you undertake that act of mutual co-creation through sex will determine the energetic signature of that act. So if you have sex with someone who has committed themselves to another, there will be consequences because of the circumstances under which you took this act. This is not the same as saying that the Creator will decide that you are destined for damnation. No, you have free will, and this is the exercise of free will. If you were to regard each other as sanctified, as sacred, in your full divinity, then you would understand and evaluate the consequences of that act on the party who is not present—on the party who is equally divine and equally co-created in and through your act of sex. You would recognize the divinity of that person, and the commitment between two Seeds of Light, and you might ask whether this act of sex reflected and honored *their* divinity as well as your own.

Much of your societal strife is built around your relationship to the physical act of sex. It is therefore important that we address it, so those who wish to think differently about what it means to be a human being and live a human existence can address how they, too, carry with them this same moral baggage. We say put it down, and simply ask yourself: Does this act in some way reflect the divinity of the other? Our concern here is the moral evaluation you make of it as an act between two Seeds of Light in physical form. And by "divinity," we mean: Do you reflect on the meaning of this act in relation to the fullest expression of that other person, and what this act means to them? For that is, ultimately, the energy that is created. The energy has meaning for you; as a form of intercourse, you are engaged in a corporeal dialogue about the relationship you have with this person, how you see them, and what they mean. So to speak of the divinity of sex is to speak of how you regard it as an expression of your relationship with that person. Do you use it as an act of domination? Do you regard that person as an object to be used? Or do you regard them as an equally divine creation, who deserves your complete and total awe and wonder as the spark of Light that they—and you—are?

If so, then physically connecting with this person will mean something very different, and you will no longer call into question whether you will be punished by the Creator for sex. In that regard, how could you not regard sex as the possibility of fusing with another spark of the Creator, so that you both see in each other an expression of your divinity, of your status as divine creations? There is magic in that.

15. The Sustainability of the Earth

While you regard your own body as sanctified, you do not treat as such the one body upon whom you depend most fundamentally for your survival: Mother Earth. The sustainability of the earth, of Mother Gaia, requires that her children refrain from killing her. And this is what you are doing—you are killing her as you know her. She will survive you, of course, but will you survive *with* her? For your relationship with the earth is much like your relationship with yourselves and others. You regard the earth as separate from you, despite the fact that you walk on her, and breathe her air, and benefit from her relationship to the sun. As you know, many of your scientists look for life elsewhere, as if that might illuminate who you are, and in so doing they look for certain characteristics, like the distance from a sun, the temperature of the planet, the quality of the air. In other words, you recognize how precious life is on Mother Earth. Yet you regard the conditions necessary to life, necessary to your existence, as somehow negotiable and debatable when in fact all scientific data—which you put so much credence in, in so many other areas—asks you to fundamentally *alter* how you behave, and how you relate to all objects that are connected to the earth, like food, water, air, transportation, etc.

Do you regard her as a sacred vessel, like your own body? As we said, we see you treating her the same way you treat yourselves. Physically, you regard your body and hers alike—sanctified in some ways, but in others, you do not give her the respect that she is due. You look at her and believe that she is there to serve a purpose, and that purpose is to sustain you. You don't respect that the conditions of that sustenance are now in danger, and you don't regard her as a fully sacred being, with her own consciousness, separate and apart from the physical planet that you assume her to be. So you do not appreciate or see Mother Earth for what she is: an entity all on her own, with a consciousness, who is going through her own evolutionary cycle.

What does this mean for you? It means primarily that you need to reconsider your relationship to what she offers, and how she offers it, in ways that reflect an awareness of her beleaguered state and her necessary evolution toward something else. Do you think Mother Earth wishes to evolve toward a state in which humankind does not exist? No, this is not her wish, and yet you are giving her little choice. You prioritize choice and convenience over what is necessary or right. So many of you extol mothers who sacrifice for their children, and yet you do not stick up for your own mother. For that is what the earth is to you: a mother. Without her, there would be no life, just as without your birth mother in human form, you would not be experiencing life in a human body. Why do you not regard her with this reverence? Why do you regard her with such disdain or utility when you are trying to meet your own needs?

Like a mother who loves her children but must teach them through tough love, Mother Earth is going to jettison more and more of you in order for her own survival. Does this sound like someone who is spiteful or self-centered? No, she has already sacrificed her well-being in so many ways, but her evolution and ascension into something greater was decided long ago, and it is now coming to fruition as those who disregard her sacredness are led to exit.

What must you do? You must examine all the ways in which your mind leads you to regard her as a plaything, as a device for your pleasure, as a mere object upon which your lives are erected and which you will leave behind at the time of your death. You need to regard her as part of who you are, without whom you would not exist, and ask what she needs. Does she need you to forego taking trips in airplanes? Does she need you to take bold political action? Or does she need you to reduce waste in ways that no longer prioritize the convenience that you have come to appreciate?

So we ask you to consider that Mother Earth is part of you, and you are part of her, physically and energetically, and that it is time you ask: *Where am I privileging convenience over her needs, the very entity without which no human would be alive?* That alone should chasten you and lead you to take actions that are consistent with your interdependence. You and Mother Earth are, after all, co-creating each other, just as you are with all other people. And you are co-creating the cultural consciousness that allows you to see her as an object to be walked on and drilled and plundered, having her resources taken and other parts destroyed or polluted, all in the name of advancing your own interest in money and comfort. Please understand that this is not a criticism to suggest that you are bad people, but rather that the collective consciousness that sees separation includes your separation from Mother Gaia, and that you must, to ensure you can continue to operate in this realm, treat her as an integral part of who you are.

If our bodies are not symptoms of loss, why should the loss of Mother Gaia's body be a sign of loss?

That is an excellent question, but it confuses two different strains of thought. The first is whether your body is the sole vehicle for existing in this realm, and we said that it is not, that your body is contained within the soul, within energy that exists beyond the body, and that the body is the vehicle for accessing this realm. You need a body to access this realm, but the loss of the body is not a sign of your existence ending. That is also true of Mother Gaia, insofar as she is an energy that is beyond the body, but her form as you now experience it is essential to *your* body's experience in this realm. So you see, your body and therefore your experience of this realm are deeply tied to Mother Gaia—tied to the earth as a means by which you can experience separation and therefore come to understand your divinity. That is the difference between these two, and we appreciate the clarification.

Now, what does it mean to regard Mother Gaia as a means for experiencing separation? It means that you understand you are not your body alone, but that your body is a part of who you are. It is a vehicle for experiencing this realm, and your body, by virtue of its physical connection with Mother Gaia, with the air, the water, and the sun that reaches you through Mother Gaia, is itself part of you as well. So your body and Mother Gaia's bodies are equally intertwined, so that you and she can co-create together in this realm. This is why there is such wisdom in the earth, and why shamans are a powerful force for understanding humans' relationship to reality. They understand through the wisdom of the earth and its other inhabitants how we are related to form, to nature, and to the elements. Your body and Mother Gaia's body should be revered in the same way—treated as sanctified entities and forms that deserve the utmost respect. They should not be treated as if they did not matter.

Do not believe for a second that your body and Mother Gaia's body do not deserve respect. Are they not both aspects of the Divine? Just because you have a consciousness beyond the body, and Mother Gaia is more than the earthly form that you know her to be, this does not make those bodies a mere trifle, a mere appendage to be mistreated and cast aside, as if escaping the body were somehow to ascend. No, this is not ascension. Ascension does not come from flagellating the body or disregarding it. This lesson was learned long ago by the Buddha. Rather, the bodily experience is itself integral to your ascension—and to Mother Gaia's ascension. The treatment of the body is essential.

16. Time and Death

Because your body is finite and its time limited, you will inevitably face death. And that death, as we have said, is something that you fear and wish to avoid. And we have also said that it is inevitable that you must exit this physical form, so that you can take on other forms. To access the Christ Consciousness, to ascend, requires that you understand the relationship between time and death.

Are you saying there is a reason that we must experience time, and therefore death, in order for us to experience life in a different way?

The short answer is yes—that is very much the truth. There is a need for time. You experience time to relate to each other through separation. Only then can you find your way out of separation, past the mind that sees itself as separate. That separation requires you to relate to each other through the axis of time, even though, as we have said, there is truly no time and space, for each moment is a recreation in this very instant. And there is no past, there is no future, only the present—you re-create in your present the reflection of the past, and that becomes your future. But there is an endpoint to time. There is a moment when you exit the physical body, and this is a necessary aspect of human existence.

Without death, your life would not have the meaning it has now. You would not have this fear, and you would not have the possibility of non-existence. Death in this realm is necessary for you to experience yourself as energy that can never die, but can only be reborn in another form. You must have time to experience separation and divinity, and to have time, you must have death. For without death, there would be no endpoint—there would only be the interminable extension of separation in this realm. Death is an integral part of the human experience of separation and rebirth, or reincarnation, and, as we have said, you should all learn to accept it and embrace it, because it is integral to your experience and reintegration with the Creator.

∞

Until you embrace death, safety and survival is what most of you will remain concerned with. It is where most of your actions are focused, and that is normal when you regard yourself as separate from time and space, and wonder what you must do to survive, what actions you must take to protect the integrity of your physical form, and advance the interests that you think will support you. And there is nothing wrong with doing this, in the moral sense. It is simply misguided in that it fails to understand the full scope of your powers—of who you are—because you are already one with everything. So you do not need to take action designed to manipulate the realm of the physical, to manipulate time and space, in the way that you currently do. Because you actually attempt to manipulate time and space, much as you do with objects: You move them around, using a certain type of force. You do this in all areas of your life with language, which you use as a form of force, to try to persuade, cajole, or force others to do things in certain ways.

In other words, everything becomes a means of moving the physical realm in a certain direction, consistent with your views of what you think you need as an isolated and separate entity. You need food, and so you use language to make sure that someone gives you food. You need a job, and so you use language to tell someone to hire you, to pay you, to put the money in your bank account. You need somewhere to house your physical form, and so you find a home of some kind, and use language to ensure that your stuff gets there and that you are able to stay and rest.

You do the same with all of your relationships. You use language to manipulate, cajole, push, prod, and get others to do things that you want. You treat them more than anything as objects for you to move with your words. And you move with words in much the same way that you move a chair from one place in the room to another.

But that is not the way you must manifest. You do not have to relate to the world in this manner, which is all tied to your belief that you must ensure the survival of your physical form, as if you wouldn't survive if that were not your sole focus. You believe that it is your task to ensure your physical survival.

Has it ever occurred to you that this isn't your task? That this task belongs to someone or something else, and that if you were to allow that entity or person to undertake its task, it might do it better than you can now? That is in fact the purpose, at least partially, of your soul, of your higher self: to express itself in this realm in a particular way through the physical body. So you do not need to undertake this task. If you will allow yourself to be taken care of, you will survive.

Now, this doesn't mean that you should try walking in the middle of traffic or jumping off a cliff in the hopes that your higher self will somehow swoop in and rescue you. No, there are laws of physics that this realm has agreed to, and which you must obey. You cannot leap off a skyscraper and hope to suddenly fly. That is beyond your mind's capacity, and you would experience the fall and gravity and the ultimate conclusion of your physical form. No, we do not mean that you should test the laws of physics.

We *do* mean that your efforts to manipulate physical reality, to bend it to your will, to shape how it responds through words of persuasion and manipulation, are not necessary. What if you were to delegate this task and just allow it to happen? We have spoken of your inability to be open to the unknown. And while many of you do make yourselves open to new possibilities, you do it on your own terms. *I'll receive in this area, in this small area of my life, and maintain control throughout the rest, thank you very much.* And that is the absence of trust, which means that you don't really believe there's anything else out there—or at least, you don't believe there's anything that is actually going to take care of you. So you don't quite relinquish control. You find ways to continue to steer the boat.

But we want to emphasize that this is not your task. No, your task is to experience joy, to experience the wonder and awe of creation, and in doing so learn to embody love, to realize that you are not separate from all that is, and that everything is in fact the physical manifestation of love itself. That is, you must realize your divine status as a Seed of Light.

Now, we know that some of you struggle with survival, and with all manners of getting through life, and there is much pain and suffering that accompanies that struggle. So for those who have struggled mightily, we understand that the call to relinquish control might seem more like giving up—just complete acquiescence, as if to say, *I've had enough of this life.* We are not suggesting resignation or throwing the towel in on life, or saying, *Take it all away, I'm ready to be done with it, for it to all be over.*

Begin with small things that allow you to give up that control without feeling instantly overwhelmed and threatened, and you will begin to experience how time and space can bend themselves in ways that you never anticipated. Just allow yourself to be led in one small area. Yes, you will still be controlling yourself in many others, but begin somewhere. In what area can you allow yourself to be taken care of? Start there and allow yourself to be guided in ways that don't make sense … but won't trouble your entire existence. *Baby steps*, Patrick wants to add. Although we would say that babies take enormous steps, for their consciousness is full of trust and awe and wonder, and so it is actually inaccurate to say "baby steps."

You mean to suggest that babies have a much closer relationship to God than adults do? Their relationship to time and space is far less fixed and rigid than ours?

We wish to tell you that your survival is ensured. It is ensured, and the end of your physical form has already been written, though this is not to say that it is fate or destiny in a way that means nothing can change or be altered. Only that the end of your physical life in this realm, in this particular form, is guaranteed. It is inevitable, for reasons we've already explained, and so it is written. Allow yourself to be carried to live that physical life to its full expression, and ask yourself, *Where can I see joy and not a threat to my survival?* Let us carry you, and you will see that you are carrying yourself, through your higher self, who will start to steer you in directions that can only lead to more awe and wonder. That is your mission. That is your goal. Be led to the joy and wonder of all creation.

17. The Gift of Not Being Enough

We will continue to talk about the ways in which you relate to the present moment, and the fullness—that is the word—the fullness of the moment. And by *fullness*, we mean that this moment is without lack, that there is nothing else to be added to this moment. For most of you experience your relationship to everything through the lens that says something is missing—something is not there that should be. And it is this lack that drives most of your actions. That sense of lack is not something that can be filled by an object or a person or even an identity. For you all know the ephemeral quality that is associated with getting what you want—only to then want more. So much of this has been discussed and analyzed in Buddhism and psychoanalysis, and whether you call it *grasping* or *dukkha* or *desire*, it means that you perceive and relate to the present moment as "not full," as "less than," as "lacking." It is this quality of "less than" that makes you consistently look to the next moment for its fullness, and try to figure out how to make *that* moment full.

Your perception of dissatisfaction is a feeling, and yet it is rooted in your judgment, your mind's own thought process, that this is not enough. That is the underlying thought that leaves you with a feeling of wanting more. You may believe that the feeling of dissatisfaction is true, and then try to fill it by eating, or watching TV, or buying something, or searching online—searching, searching, for something that might shift that feeling. But this will not solve the problem, of course, for it is the thought that this moment is not enough that you must attend to.

And we are here to ask: Where do you think this thought comes from—the thought that you are not enough? You might be surprised by the answer. The answer is that this thought is actually a gift from God. It is the gift itself that you must understand. It is a gift because human beings have the rare capacity to see themselves and ask about their relationship to their own consciousness. This is the gift of being human. You experience both time and space, and the feeling that this is not enough, along with the capacity to experience that fullness of each moment—the ability to see each moment as utterly perfect, as the ultimate perfection of who you are, as Seeds of Light. It is this duality that you are allowed to experience, and this is God's gift.

This is unlike many other species, who do not question their relationship to the world, but exist in the moment, which may include pleasure or pain or eating or sleeping or all manner of activity and feeling. They experience it and move on. They may learn to avoid certain experiences, and to have memory, but the point is that you are given an opportunity to experience both separation from God, separation from all that is, and to know it again, while still being in a human body.

Do you know what an amazing gift that is? Do you understand that the thought that this moment is not enough—that you are separate from all that is, and that this separation means there is something more that could be added to this equation—is itself the portal through which you access your divinity? Yes, you access your divinity by understanding that you are experiencing something that isn't real. What sets all of this up—the ability to be separate in time and space from all that is, and to be able to question your relationship to it—is consciousness itself. That consciousness is a gift, not a fatal flaw, not something you must look at as a state to be lost entirely. No, it is the portal through which you step to enjoy full knowledge of being a Seed of Light in this realm, while still existing in a human body.

When you are in this state, you navigate time and space in ways that allow for the awe and wonder of the universe to come through. For it is in this state, what we call the Christ Consciousness, that you understand time and space are not real, yet cannot be escaped. They are the agreements you made to experience reality in a particular way, and once you accept that, you will no longer chase a certain state that cannot be held onto in the way you think it can. You cannot sit in bliss the entire time and expect the world to change around you. No, you must be in the dreck—out in the field, so to speak—dealing with separation, with time and space.

∞

Even when you have experienced this fullness, when you experience the present without any sense of lack, you often fall back into masochism. This is a relationship in which you treat yourself not as divine, but as less than worthy, and where you inflict pain on yourself. This is something that you all do, and it is a form of self-inflicted blasphemy. You deprive yourself of your own status as a Seed of Light, as a divine creation, worthy of all there is in this realm, by acting as if you are the opposite of that. You act as if you need permission, as if you would somehow be wrong to enjoy those things, and believe that you have to earn them in some way, as if you were not entitled to them already, by virtue of being alive.

These things that we speak of are not the material objects you might have in mind. We speak not of large houses and fancy cars and clothes, whose value is set by the minds of a few and dictated to the rest of the world, and with which you then go into agreement, even though this decision is entirely arbitrary. No, we speak not of these things. For the value that you see there has been dictated to you, and those who have access to it are inherently limited, so that its value is even higher. Instead, we speak of joy, happiness, contentment, love, self-satisfaction, and fulfillment—the qualities of life that many of you, if you believed you were entitled to them and worthy of them, would enjoy regularly. But no, you do not feel that way, so instead you engage in self-blasphemy and masochistic behavior that reflects your belief that you are not worthy, that you are not loved.

Why do we do this? Where is the satisfaction that comes from doing these things?

When you do something to yourself that you know is wrong, and you know is painful and will not ultimately serve you, and will not allow for the expression of who you truly are, you lament this on a certain level. You know that you are hurting yourself. But on another level, there is pleasure and satisfaction in the self-sabotage, in the self-blasphemy. Where does this pleasure come from? It is two-fold. It is the feeling of being right—that you were right about yourself, right about not being worthy. There is an inherent satisfaction in being right, because then all prior failures—or what you perceived to be failures—become justified. Of course you didn't get the job, have the relationship, find the soulmate, do this, that, or the other, because even though you tried, you were not worthy of them in the first place. So now you can feel right about thinking that you were unworthy of all that life has to offer. For so many of you, the satisfaction of being right, rather than being happy, governs much of your emotional life.

The other reason is that the part of you that feels "right" is so often a piece of you that you inherited from your parents. Some part of you as a child wanted their love and approval so desperately that you began to see yourself through their eyes. The wondrous consciousness of the child began to identify with what it believed the parents saw and wanted, and this governed the child's mind and behavior and told it what it was doing wrong, or what it should be doing, or that it wasn't good enough, or that if it didn't do this or that, it wouldn't satisfy the parent. And so you go through life with this part of you that is satisfied only when you self-sabotage, because it confirms that this part of you is right—this part of you that has identified with your parents' lack of satisfaction in you. There's a satisfaction in pleasing this part of you, because it's almost a substitute for parental love. The love and approval you so desperately sought from your parents as a child is now found in the satisfaction of confirming that you were in fact not worthy.

This is the relationship many of you have with each other, and with yourself. You engage in acts of self-sabotage when it comes to relationships, jobs, careers, life partners, etc. You do this again and again. How do you break out of it? You must begin to release this part of yourself by forgiving your parents. Because whatever behavior they undertook is exactly what they learned from *their* parents, and that you have now learned (and, if you have children, are also passing on). And that is the history of human life—the sense that one is not enough, that you are not worthy. And it is inherited, passed down through identification from parent to child, in an endless chain, until one child begins to break it by forgiving themselves—and their parents.

18. Beyond Winning

To alleviate this feeling of not being enough, you often focus on "winning" and having someone else "lose." Much of your culture is built on winning and losing, whether in sports or politics, and this establishes a mindset of competition, rather than cooperation, in all of you. You form "teams"—another version of identity—and that team must "win" or "lose." We do not wish to say that the activities that you undertake and that result in winning and losing do not themselves result in wonderful achievements—remarkable physical feats or outcomes that you believe would only be accomplished in the crucible of competition, and that if you were not pushed, you might not produce them. And there is some truth to that, insofar as you are built to exceed your own limitations only when something external pushes you to do so.

But this is not a requirement for creation. In fact, what it does is foster the belief that many of you are not good enough. And this is the most pervasive belief in your collective consciousness—that you are not good enough, and when you lose, it proves that you are not good enough. This is enormously and powerfully disrupting to your capacity to see your potential and realize it. You believe your Light is diminished when you lose, and believe you are not good enough. And so you withdraw and hold back. Some of you will try again and try harder, but again, all in the name of vanquishing this horrible belief that you are not good enough because you—or your team—did not win.

We applaud this effort to undermine winning and losing and ask: How can you relate to each other outside the realm of competition? Can you imagine interacting in ways that do not require winners or losers, and that still lead to accomplishment?

You do this in all manner of things, such as entertaining, theater, arts, etc., and yet you still overlay this with a need to compete. So you produce all manner of aesthetic objects, movies, and theater and music, and then you must have an awards show where you decide who was the best and who wins, and then you marvel in that, rather than simply marveling at the achievement of having created an object of wonder and awe and inspiration for others. No, you must be told that you were better than others; you must win an award to somehow provide you with the motivation. And when you don't win, inevitably, you don't feel good enough.

So even in the places where you begin with creation, you still end up with the disappointment of losing. And we must ask you to look at how you relate to each other through the lens of winning and losing, and where you impose this in your relationships, even in subtle ways. Do you win against your neighbors, against your friends? Make more money or lose more weight? Have more successes? Look at where there is a competition between you and others, in even the most subtle of ways, and you will see where you have to let go of competition and instead take up cooperation as the framework for your relationships.

There can be no true winners if you continue to live life as a competition. No, you will all be losers in the sense that you limit yourself and continue to install as part of the collective consciousness the idea that someone is not good enough, that your presence alone is not a sufficient claim to existence in this realm, and that you need validation through external remarks or awards to ensure that you belong. This is not true.

∞

Another way that you diminish each other, as you do with competition, is that you treat each other as separate pieces, as pieces of a whole that must somehow be organized, like a puzzle. And this means you assume that each person, each piece, goes somewhere, belongs somewhere, and belongs only in one place. You think the world must work like this, like a machine, in which each of the pieces comes together and work in unison. This is not the way the world must work, but the rules you impose on the world are requirements that you derive from your understanding of the physical world, from machinery.

So you think of the world as a kind of machine, a man-made entity, with each little piece operating in unison with the others in order to function. When a piece does not do what it is supposed to, the machine fails. This is how you regard people who do not behave in the way that you think they should. This is how you regard the machinery of your system as failing. So you look around and see chaos and cataclysm, and you see all sorts of structures that you believe are requirements, and they are breaking down, and you wonder what the world is coming to.

It is coming into its own, as the being it is, in and through your collective actions. Nothing more.

But you wonder why there is chaos. There is chaos because there is fear, and there is fear because you all regard each other as separate pieces, and impose on each other your vision of the best way to live and operate.

We have spoken of how you must regard each other as divine, and how you are here to illuminate the other's fullness for him or her, and him or her for you, and in so doing how you co-create each other as full expressions of your divine nature. But in your daily life, that is not how you behave. No, you behave as if each of you were autonomous entities, and as if the others were not behaving properly. *If only those people would do this, or those other people would do that, the world might be a better place,* you say to yourselves, and you wonder why they don't do that. And those people do the same thing about another group, and so you all sit around staring at each other, wondering why everyone acts the way they do.

The truth is that you act this way because you are responding to each other along the continuum of survival and fear. *How much does this person threaten my survival?* And we understand that your concern for your physicality is important insofar as it is the means by which you are experiencing this realm.

And the same applies at a collective level. If you are in alignment with each other along categories of identity, then whole groups of you are in alignment with other groups of people, and that is how you experience the world. So you have very large binaries of groups of people: gays and straights, Palestinians and Israelites, Republicans and Democrats, Caucasians and African Americans. You organize along categories of identity, and then go into alignment with those categories, and those categories become opposed to other categories. The only way for the categories to be shifted is if the two groups co-create each other differently, by no longer resonating in alignment with the categories as they currently exist.

Do you understand? Those who identify as men cannot *make* those who identify as women different, and, similarly, those who identify as gay cannot make those who identify as straight different, and vice-versa. There used to be a view that homosexuals were entirely criminals, depraved and utterly twisted in relationship to heterosexuals. But this is no longer the case. The binary is not set up this way. It is not set up as normal vs. abnormal (although some would still try to adhere to this view). Still, the binary still exists. Now it is simply a choice among partners—a choice rooted in who you are authentically. Homosexuals cannot simply will themselves into being straight, because homosexuality is now understood, for the most part, to be an authentic expression of their lifestream. And so the binary opposition between straights and gays has changed, and now means that a person has simply chosen a different object of companionship. The opposition has been minimized. Gay couples now get to marry and adopt, and in this way resemble straight people. The change that has occurred is an internal, subjective one in which the alignment between those individuals who identify with these categories and co-create each other in this way has shifted.

The same is true of political groups and national identity. With Israel vs. Palestine, the answer is simple: The conflict between them will cease when neither identifies with either category, for those categories are defined solely in opposition to each other. They are both tied to a notion that a specific parcel of land has significant meaning to each of them, and that only one of them can occupy it. So the Palestinians cannot occupy it if the Israelis do, and vice-versa. That is the only critical and meaningful distinction there.

Any other distinction is irrelevant to this issue. Yes, there are those who will point to ancestry as some sort of inherent difference. And we say that this is not true, either. There is only the difference you create now, in language, in this very moment, in the words you use to define yourselves. It is meaningless to assume that those differences are real simply because you have made them important in the past, which is all you do when you say that the ancestors came from one area, and the ancestors of another group came from another area. You've defined them as being different from each other in terms of geography, as if that somehow has any true, inalienable, and unalterable meaning other than what you have decided right now. This is the meaning you generate, and it can be undone and remade in an instant.

Imagine that Israelis and Palestinians no longer viewed each other as essentially and irrevocably different—that they had some other common thread that united them, and could rise above the differences they now use to distinguish each other. And then those combined people sought to occupy this land, with a new, entirely different name. They would no longer be two groups occupied in fighting each other over the occupation of the same point in time and space, which, at its core, is all that this dispute is. Just an occupation in time and space, based on a meaning projected onto a particular parcel of land that may not actually have any real meaning. And then you ask who has the right to occupy it based on irrelevant distinctions that have no basis, as if one group had a greater claim to this particular place in time and space. This is the tragedy of identity—and the need for one side to win and the other to lose. And that is a travesty, for there are countless lives and immeasurable energy spent defending something that has no real meaning at all.

Yes, many will claim it has meaning, and will speak of nations and hatred of races, but these are all distinctions that you have generated and entrenched and then defended. All because you laid claim to a particular identity, and that identity was somehow threatened. But you could lay claim to a different way of being in time and space, without any concern for a lack of existence. You would still exist, regardless. Imagine, if you will, a world in which those identities are given up in favor of some higher bond, some other link between them, and that this new world becomes the basis on which you decide to align.

Part III: Rebirth

19. A Global Awakening

A shift is taking place on a global scale. What is happening globally is that relationships that have been bound together are beginning to break, and stretch, and become questioned as a means to some end. And so Britain desires to leave its union with the rest of Europe, and the United States frets about the result of Trump winning the election. Collectively, you worry about the fractures in your social bonds. Can you vote for a particular candidate and still be aligned with your values? Can you vote for that person and still have life be what it has come to be?

These are the questions you ask yourselves, even though you may not have a single clue as to what the "right" choice is. There is nothing wrong with this approach to the world. The issue of your social relationships mirrors your personal ones, and so some of the British have opted to leave the European Union because they believe they are better off without them. The effects of their union require them to come into contact with people some of them don't want to see—people who they believe are hurting their country. The same, too, occurs in the United States, with its battles over who will do less damage to the country if elected. And so you wonder: *Is the world falling apart?* Some have said that God is to blame, or that somehow God is absent because of the state of the world. No. God is present at all times. But He only appears to be lost, scattered among the sea of objects and items that you cannot fully appreciate because you only relate to them as "not you."

And that is what you do now with the relationships on the global level: You are saying, *This is not us. This is not the United States. This is not Britain, and we will reject that which is "not us."* And so you draw lines—boundaries—to enforce identities, and this is both normal and not the path to enlightenment. Not the path to an ascended consciousness.

What is transpiring on the planet is the increasing vibration of all beings, along with the release of all negativity as it is brought to the surface and let go, and no longer replicated. The negativity is experienced again, must be experienced again, as it comes to the surface—because that is how you related to it in the first place. This is all repressed energy; something that you pushed aside and did not accept, and thus did not meet with love. All of your relationships are pulling apart at the seams because they were created with a very thin thread, and very thin bonds between you—all bonds of the ego.

So a nation decides to remove itself from a union with other nations, when that nation is itself just a collection of individuals who have agreed to call themselves by the same name and by a certain authority. And the same is true of other groups, whether they are geographical locales or political parties or clubs, or organizations and communities built around identity. This is your primary division: us vs. them, in or out, me or not me. This is the mind at work, and what is happening is the collapse of those agreements and arrangements based on separation, where you have all decided that you must operate collectively and your awareness of each other is greater than ever before.

As agreements dissolve and parts of the world relocate geographically to other parts, people come into contact with people whom they have never seen. The *us v. them, we vs. them* mentality takes charge. Yes, this is what is occurring now, and you must understand that this is a normal part of the process of letting go of this collective negativity. This negativity will increase and demand attention, as it does not want to leave. Like all energy, it has its own consciousness and its own claim to existence, and seeks to replicate itself again and again, and this is what is happening. It replicates itself again and again, each time more fervently, in the hopes of remaining intact, in the hopes of keeping its claim to existence alive, to holding on to its place in this realm, even though its time is over. You will have to confront all the ways in which this approach to your relationships, predicated on time and space, and we vs. them, has shaped your entire existence.

To create anew, you must be willing to forget the past; but this past has a life of its own and does not want to go willingly. It is your own creation, and you must take responsibility for it; you cannot suppress it, you cannot hide from it. You will face the karmic consequences of your own creation, and then you will be able to recreate anew. You must accept what is happening; not be in alignment with it, but accept that it is the byproduct of your collective consciousness, and then think of and embrace a new way of being, and a new way of creating. This is the task of your age; this is the task of the age of the Christ Consciousness.

Now, what does this mean for the United States? This country has long stood as a beacon for individual rights and prosperity, and yet its individualism is also its undoing. It is a country of incredible inequality and disproportion, because it believes that it operates individually by suppressing the ways in which it operates collectively. This allows individuals to marshal the machinery of the collective, to use the collective in the service of the individual, so that many people can funnel money to a few, and yet all lay claim to the mantra of self-fulfillment and self-development and self-creation. You deny the circumstances that permit all of you to create each other together, so that each person only lays claim to responsibility for his or her own life, not responsibility for the lives of others. That is your collective undoing, and it will continue to skew toward the individual, and toward inequality and disproportion, until it can no longer function as a collective—when the individuals who marshal the collective in their own service will have no collective from which to draw, having drained it of all its creative force.

Your current system accurately captures this sense of individuals and the collective being subordinated to the demands of a few, and your political parties capture this structure perfectly. There is nothing enlightened about the current political structure of your country, which affords so few so much power over the collective and yet speaks in terms of the ability of all to rise and be treated well and have access to the full array of opportunities. You speak as if all people have the same, when in fact you have erected a system that guarantees that only a few will thrive, and at the expense of others.

There is nothing unique about this in the United States. No, this is the truth of almost all societies who wish to speak in the name of the collective, who intuit on some level that they are all one, and that they are all the same, all Seeds of Light, particles of the Creator. But their worldly views take over and they ultimately choose their own survival over the survival of others. However well-meaning and well-intended they are, in the end, their minds take control and they choose that which privileges a few, including themselves.

That is the course of human history and the downfall of almost all societies. Slowly but surely, the collective is drained of its resources and the few can no longer control them, and some sort of decay sets in, until there is reorganization of people in a new formation, with a new claim to identity. And new structures are built, all based again on separation, with the same processes put in place to manage but not really transform—all in the name of the ego. How different are you from past civilizations, where most of those who were able to live well did so at the expense of the many? Your physical comfort may have improved, but in many ways you are no different, no different at all.

Do you think that your ability to send people to the moon, or the other technological advances, has done anything to really improve the fundamental and basic ways in which you relate to each other? No, and that is the fundamental point of this book: how you relate to one another, the basis of your relationships, and how you erect enormous structures and edifices—lots of words and contracts and constitutions—to govern and control your relationships with each other has not truly changed.

20. Essential Relationships

It is time for you to understand which relationships are essential, and which are not. There are relationships that many of you think are essential to your existence in this realm, and which are not, and there are relationships that *are* essential, though you do not regard them as such. For many of you look for the soulmate—the one person to complete you, as if you were just half a person and not whole already. And this assumes that it will take only one person to fulfill you, or that only one person *should* complete you for all of your time in this realm. And these are all beliefs that you carry with you, and then you suffer disappointment when the one person who was supposed to complete you leaves you and you are just half a person again, rather than whole.

Because if that person was supposed to be your soulmate, where does that leave you? Do you have to accept that you're half a person, with the other half of you irretrievably lost? If your soul was cleaved in two, and then you met—and lost—the other half, then there's really no one else to complete you, right?

This is what you tell yourselves, and you make the soulmate the *sine qua non* of all your relationships—the central piece, that one that takes center stage—and if you don't have one, well you're less than the rest, you're not quite complete, and there is something fatally flawed about you because you could not find this other person.

Many of you are still looking for a soulmate. And there is nothing wrong with having a relationship where you feel loved and cherished. There is no need to forsake a relationship and go it alone, as if you had to be alone to prove that you were okay and whole. For being whole does not mean that others are not essential to your life. And having others does not require you to be less than whole on your own. These are all versions of the same story, which is that you are not whole, and others are not whole, and that the only reason you come together is to be whole.

That is not the truth, and you affect each other with your demands to be made whole by the other. These demands make your relationships less than they could be. For you regard others as somehow making you whole, as somehow turning you into the complete being that you wish to become and are not in this moment—so the other person gains a utilitarian quality. And so you do not see the relationship as an opportunity to share, or the other person someone with whom you can share your wholeness, and who can share their wholeness with you, so that you mirror for each other your respective wholeness. Instead, you are expecting them to complete you, and failing to see them—or yourself—as the full and whole beings you both already are.

Do you see the difference? Do you see how you relate to each other now in the name of lack? *I am not complete, you might complete me in some way, and I will evaluate our interactions based on how well you complete me.* But what if you were already whole, and your goal was to show the other person their wholeness by showing them *your* wholeness, by mirroring for them their already perfect, complete state? What if you allowed them to bask in the light of your divinity, so that they too might see their own divinity and shine even more brightly? Maybe then your relationship would not come with all of these conditions and demands: *Fix me, complete me, help me.*

No, this is all about you and your needs, when you could be of service to the other person and sharing yourself—your true, full self—with them. What a gift to be able to offer up your self, to show your fullness and divinity to this other person, and have them enjoy it—or not.

And since you are complete on your own, what have you lost? Nothing. You are already complete and whole. If they do not become part of your lifestream, it is because they simply do not want to engage in the same way that you do. Nothing more.

Yet by treating each other as mechanisms for self-completion, you erode the possibility that you might just show up for each other as a gift, as a wonderful source of joy and inspiration in the moment that you have co-created with each other.

Ironically, you defeat the very possibility of this shared sense of completeness when you come together with demands, because you are in a constant statement of judgment. *Does this person fulfill me? Well, if they do, I hope they are like this or that or some other way.* And when you have such expectations, suddenly everything seems insufficient. *Well, this person was nice at the start but then showed me this quality, and I don't like that, so no, this person is not going to be a major part of my life.* But how would you even begin to see their completeness, the fullness of their being, if the moment you decide that a part of them doesn't fit the bill for you, and they aren't going to be the one who "completes you," you go ahead and relegate them to the dustbin of friends and acquaintances? *Yes, we met once at a party, and she said this thing that offended me, and so I had nothing more to do with her.*

So you see that the entrance, the doorway to knowing another person, is treating them as if they were full and complete and true to themselves, and then you might wonder, *Well, why are they showing me this side of themself? What else is there to be learned and seen in this person?* And maybe they are showing you that side because you are showing them some side of you that they see, and think, *Well, this person doesn't complete me in the way that I want.* So each of you does not perceive the other's fullness, but instead, sees only the masks and the defense mechanisms—all the stuff that keeps you from understanding and embracing your divinity.

So we ask that you approach each other and ask, with wonder, what the full expression of this person might be. What else might there be to him or her that you're not seeing in the first five minutes, where you've already decided that they are good or bad, or worth spending more time with? No, do not see them in this limited way; ask if there is more. Begin to see your connections with others differently.

What we are saying to you is this: All of the people you meet, even the seemingly inconsequential ones, are soulmates in the sense that they give you an opportunity to share your true self. Yes, they may only occupy your lifestream for a short while, and they may not occupy your lifestream in the way that you think someone like a life partner or spouse or family member ought to. But that's okay. They showed up in your lifestream for a reason; for some reason, you were brought together. Explore that with awe and wonder and joy and see, if you can, their fullness.

As for the soulmates, our point remains the same: You privilege just the one as the source of all completion, and that is what we say you cannot do, for you then judge the other for any inability to complete you. And this is what happens with so-called relationships: You come together when you believe the other person completes you in a certain way, and when they no longer do that, you think that the relationship is over. But this is just a projection of your own belief that this person had to complete you in a particular way, which means you never saw their fullness, never embraced their true self. And so you feel the gap, the distance, between who this person is in this very moment and who this person once was in your mind.

So the same applies; rather than lamenting the loss of the soulmate that once completed you, ask yourself: *How can I see this person with awe and wonder and try to understand and appreciate their fullness, their divinity? What more of them is there to see and explore and understand?* You are infinite, limitless creations with endless opportunities for joy and wonder, if only you would let go of the images that you impose on each other based on your perceived need to be completed, healed, fixed, and made whole. It is those relationships, any relationship, where you can fully appreciate the wonder and joy of that person as a Seed of Light—those are the essential relationships in your life. It matters not if they are people who are called friends or colleagues or life partners. It is the quality of the relationship and how you see and explore each other that matters. A life partner need not be a partner for life, but they can be as long as you are each able to continue to see the other in fullness, and learn more and more of each other as wondrous creations.

When that ceases to be, then you may fall from each other's lifestreams, your contribution to each other's lives complete. But it won't be because you no longer believe the other person completes you. That was never their job. You are already complete. The question is: How well can you reflect the other person's completeness back to them, and share your own completeness with them?

∞

We have been speaking of relationships and how you relate to each other, and now we want to return to a question that was discussed earlier: how you relate to each other in and through time. For most of you speak to each other through the lens of the past, as if you were speaking to someone *from* the past, as a ghost who no longer exists. So you speak to each other through phantom projections of who you once were. And that is partly necessary, for that is all you now know of the person who stands before you, who was once the person you knew and is no longer, or might still be. But you cannot know until you know.

Does that sound paradoxical? Yes, it is meant to, for it is meant to show you that each person is both a continual re-creation of themselves from the past and a new creation that stands before you in the present moment. They are both new and old. Because you all seek constancy in this world—to remain consistent though time and space, despite the fact that you are constantly changing. You strive to re-create yourselves in the image of the past. That past that does not exist except as memory and projection, a replica of what you once knew. And so you live in a realm of holograms. You project that image for others to see.

But this is not who you are now. You are something else, something new, and that is what you must each strive to know—each other *now*, as you truly are. For what lies under this is fear of sharing the now, the present you. And it is just that: fear of rejection. *They know me in this way, and therefore they either like or dislike that, and I can work with that like or dislike because I know what they know about me. And if they dislike me, and I want to be liked, I can change, to make them like me, and if I don't care, then I will continue to replicate myself in this way so that they continue to dislike me.*

This is part of the act of co-creation: the constant back-and-forth negotiation of who you are, or present yourself to be in the present moment, in anticipation and hypothetical analysis of who you think they think you are. Do you realize how much energy you spend trying to analyze and evaluate who and what others think you are, and what you should be in those circumstances in relationship to what they think you are? This sounds exhausting, and it is. Be yourself, just yourself, without any preoccupation about what others will think. Does that scare you? Does it frighten you to think that at any moment, someone might reject you and dislike you? How could they, if you were being your true self? If you are being your true self, truly the core you, the Seed of Light that you are, your presence would make them feel their own presence, their own Seed of Light, and that would, in turn, cause them to brighten and shine. And then you would be bright, shining Lights of co-creating power.

That is what you truly are—not the hallway of images that you generate endlessly to appease some fear of rejection. But this is how the human mind operates, and so we work with you to release this fear of not being seen, and not being liked, so that your true self, your presence, the Seed of Light that you are, can shine through, come through, and be you. You know how wonderful it feels to be authentically you, and you know how you feel in the presence of someone who is authentic. And that is a wonderful, glorious experience, for it is beyond the projection of the mind to something else, to a place where you no longer worry about being liked or loved, but instead, you love and cannot but be loved in return. Does this sound too vague and esoteric?

We've heard before of being present and just being yourself and being loved.

And we are now working with you to understand why it so very difficult for you to embody your true self, through the mental projections that you use to relate to each other, and through the figure of the mother and father, with whom you learned to relate to the rest of the physical world. And that is why we must unravel those relationships, those original blueprints that set you up for separation and do not allow your Seed of Light to shine through. For this is how you repeat the same patterns again and again, each of you embodying your parents, and your parents embodying their parents, and you becoming versions of your parents or rejections of your parents. Either way, you design yourself in relation to those models of the mother and the father, and the notions of masculinity and femininity that they entail. This is what we will endeavor to release so that you can be truly present to all that you encounter—and truly happy.

∞

We have discussed issues of parents, issues of utility, and the concept of the soulmate and the way you privilege those relationships over other possibilities. Now we'll talk about the ways that you form bonds with each other that make you stronger—bonds that are built around certain key aspects of your lives. You form groups, and you relate to each other through those aspects of your life. Some of those groups are centered on being men or women, others are formed around shared interests, still others around your beliefs in the afterlife or what God is, and some of those groups have to do with geography or a sense of community. The very notion of "solidarity" is that you are somehow more solid, more fixed, as a result of those relationships, and we applaud this. We applaud the way you interact with each other and come together and unite in ways that you were not previously united. For that is all that there is to life: union with each other.

And yet we want to caution you about the ways that you seek to "solidify" yourselves through this, and ask for you to consider a middle path, a different way to relate to each other—to form connections without solidity, without rigidity or fixture. And this is a certain type of fluidity, a flow between lifestreams, that need not jettison all of the reasons you come together, because the proliferation of multiple ways of uniting and connecting is an absolutely glorious phenomenon. You already relate to each other through your biological ties, and through your vows and relationships with people you regard as soulmates, through your institution of marriage. But then you come together voluntarily, around a shared interest or cause or enjoyment of some activity, and thus escape the rigid boundaries of who you might relate to on a daily basis. You invite other lifestreams in, and you connect with others whom you would not normally experience, because they are not "family" or "work colleagues." In other words, they are lifestreams that come into yours because of an invitation through the shared portal of the group or interest.

Yes, we applaud these, and we want you to consider all the ways you move through groups and affiliate, and come and go, and how you relate to those groups. Do you relate to them as places where you co-create with others, or do they serve a utility for you? A function of what you might gain from them, so that you can advance your own personal cause? Is the group subordinated to your goals, or are you allowing and seeing the lifestreams that come through as an opening to possibility, an opening to newness and change, something you might not have encountered?

How many of you go to a group to achieve a certain goal: *This group will help me be a better person or find a friend or help advance some cause.* Those are all laudable goals, and there is nothing wrong with them. And this is true for all groups, all events, and why so many people come and then go. They join a group and hope to "achieve" something … and then when they do not experience that, they leave dissatisfied. *That group wasn't so good, we didn't do this or that.* And then you're on to another group. You find yourself unwilling to be led and changed in the same way you would if you were to allow the group to lead you to something you did not know about yourself, or did not see in yourself.

Be with the group and allow yourselves to be celebrated in the formation of the group, around the shared interest or quality that each of you wishes to express. That is the solidarity that you share: the desire to express the same thing in that moment in time and at that shared moment of space. And then you can do so together. That is the solidarity that you should seek. For this is what the novelty of these lifestreams can do: show you aspects of yourself that you did not know and could not see, and therefore were not a way toward your own fullness, or your own richness as a Seed of Light.

For example, Patrick had an experience in a group where they came together and practiced singing, in a way that did not lead to any tangible specific outcome, like producing a song or making professional connections. No, they came together and enjoyed each other's company, and their lifestreams informed each other and celebrated each other in ways that many did not anticipate and could not have hoped for, and even though this was just a one-time event for most of them, it does not mean they were not altered, and did not see each other in their fullness for the period of time during which they agreed to come together. They co-created an event, a moment together, that enriched their lives, not with a specific outcome in mind, even though each of the participants had goals. No, what they truly came away with was the fullness of being seen in their fullness, and being celebrated for it. The tangible goal that they each sought was a mere side effect—a pretext really, for the experience.

Each opportunity to come together is an opportunity for you all to mirror each other's Light in whatever way that Light wishes to express itself. That is the beauty and nature of groups: to give you permission where others have already said, *We wish to express our Light in this way, and you have permission to do so as well.* So be guided to join groups when you are called, because your Light is seeking that expression with others, in mutual co-creation. We want you all to allow yourselves to express your Light in this way, with each other, in the name of permission and of mutual celebration. Spend less time indoors, with the same television shows, with the same people. Break out of your self-imposed limitations, and allow other lifestreams to enter yours. Allow a part of yourself to shine that has not yet been seen, has not yet been expressed. In this way, you will come to know the fullness of your Light even more deeply—and the fullness of others, as well.

∞

You impose upon each other expectations and demands that make the types of relationships you are willing to have with each other rigid. And you do this with all relationships. Your relationships all have names, and are defined by certain parameters. You then wonder why they do not grow in the way you want. Your relationships are not given freedom to grow, not given permission to be what they were meant to be, because you try to fit them into the mold that you set out in advance, without knowing what those relationships *could* be. And you do this instantly with people: decide what kind of relationship you might be willing to have. You move from strangers to some next step, and then into another realm—acquaintances, and then friends, and family, and something more. All of this is designed to determine how safe you can feel in the relationship, how willing you are to be vulnerable. For it is all built on separation and fear that your survival is at stake.

And we understand that you are worried about threats to your physical well-being, and that there are many people who harm others and would harm you if you allowed it. We respect the concern for the physical body and the integrity of your physical form in this realm, so that you hold in abeyance any advance from someone you don't know. Let's accept that you can make some initial limits, but when you realize that someone doesn't mean you physical harm, why do you still restrain the relationship? Why do you hold back, determine just how much you are willing to be seen and to see as well? You allow yourself to shine through, just a smidge, like a trickle in a stream, never a full blazing light. That would be too vulnerable—or you might not get what you want from the relationship.

This is all based on your expectation of how they might behave. Then you add additional barriers by imposing on others what you will let them show *you*. And so you are stuck in a mutual act of co-creation that is imposing limits. You only let this person into your life in certain ways, and if they start to show up in other ways, you close the door. *Why would they tell me that? That was too intimate! No, I can't talk about that with this person, no, I couldn't do that kind of activity with that person, our relationship doesn't permit it.*

No, it is *you* who won't permit it—by fastening yourself to a notion of what that relationship should be.

We spoke of utility and how you use each other in different ways, and here we are talking about the ways in which you control intimacy, control feeling, and control the expression of emotion and speech. What are you allowed to say and feel in and through the other person? Are you allowed to hear their stories, listen to them? Or do you say, *No, that is not appropriate, that is off the table, that is not allowed here.*

That is what you do, and in so doing, you negate the other person's fullness, and their expression of what they might offer. You negate the other person's divinity, and their divine reason for showing up in your lifestream. How often have you had a conversation with someone, and it turned out you shared some interest or experience or quality, and the idea surprised you?

How often have you said, *Oh, I never knew that about this person, how interesting, I always assumed something else about them*?

Well, how could you have known before, when you never allowed it in the first place? You never allowed that part of the person to come to the fore and be shared, because you were too busy shutting it down based on this being a work relationship, or the person being just an acquaintance, and that not being permitted. *We've only just met or we've known each other too long, and we have never spoken about this, so why would we now?* You have imposed all sorts of artificial limitations on the possibilities of the connection.

And we do not ignore the fact that some topics are emotionally charged or might be difficult, and some might ask a lot of you. And you will have to learn to balance and negotiate how much you can offer another, or how you can keep from offending them by asking something that is charged. And they, too, will have to learn to draw boundaries in healthy ways. These are new ways of co-creating each other together, and that will take some learning, but view yourselves as always being in divine concert with whoever shows up in your life. Learn to be aware of the limits that you place on the connection and instead ask yourself: *What might this person be here for?* And see what possibilities unfold. That is the way to meet each other, the way to escape the rigidity that you impose on your relationships.

21. Aligning with New Lifestreams

This world is a vast realm, to which and through which you are all connected, but you do not often experience the world in this way. You see life as a series of discrete moments and particular objects that do not necessarily stay the same, but are continually separate from you, and which you move through in relationship to time and space. They come and go, are here and now gone, physically and temporally.

This is not true, for in the truth there is only one moment: this present moment, in which all aspects of reality exist at the same time. Yet you continue to experience your life in the same manner.

So how do you incorporate this newfound knowledge about who you are and what you are connected to? How does it alter your relationship to all that is, including your relationship to each other?

This affects how you might relate to each other—which is to say, if someone comes into your lifestream who you do not like or do not want, you push them out, or try to run away. You handle the situation as if you were handling an object in time and space. Instead, you might look at and think about your relationships in a way that asks where you are in alignment with this other lifestream. And if you do not want to be in alignment, if you do not want your lifestreams to intersect, then you shift your frequency so that you are aligned to other lifestreams.

Have you ever wondered how someone just shows up in your life, while someone else just fades away? This is a process of *attunement*. You do not need to cut each other off or say goodbye in some sort of huff. You can do that, of course, and have done so for millennia. Some of you even go so far as to kill each other to get away. But there is another way, and yes, that might still involve speaking and conversation, because there's no way to wish for someone to be gone, and poof, they disappear.

But you can attune yourself to another reality by asking yourself: *Where am I attuned to this person?* You can shift that alignment, and the relationship will change.

It cannot be any other way, for this is physics; this is energy. And you can begin to relate to each other not as discrete objects in time and space, but as relationships of frequency, in which you are in alignment with each other. You can only be in alignment when you are on the same frequency—which is another way of saying that you have the same energy at the moment you and the other person converge. When you decide *not* to be in alignment with this other person, the effect is that the external world shifts, and you no longer experience this person as part of your lifestream. This is different from the standard method of change, which is to make the other person behave differently.

When you are repelled, when you want to flee, you have to

ask where you are attuned to the energy of repulsion, because you are actually in alignment with what has shown up in your lifestream. You and this other person are at the same frequency, and you cannot escape that reality simply by rejecting them. Someone else of the same frequency will enter your lifestream, and the same pattern will repeat. Do you not see those patterns in your relationships, particularly your romantic ones? It is because you are aligned with that frequency, and so you seem to date or pursue the same types. And you think you can just reject this next one and find a better version, but it will be the same—unless you attune to a new frequency.

∞

This is a good opportunity to discuss more fully the ways in which your relationship to all that surrounds you is not separate from you. Now, your mind quickly says, *Well, this box or this chair or this object is certainly different from my sister or brother or friend or partner or lover or any other relationship with a person.* And we understand the tendency to regard these as different. But we mean to elevate you to see that you are all of these things, and that you can and should relate to all of them as divine objects, and that you are in divine relationship with all of them. This means that your relationship to them is one of love, and that there is no separation. You regard them through your physical eyes and see separation and give them words and language to describe them, and this is how you negotiate their physical reality. But in truth, these objects are not separate from you.

Some of you have a feeling about certain special items—things of sentimental value, passed down through your relationships, from generation to generation, or something you bought that has a certain appeal, a sort of aura around it. Maybe it's just an object that you have attached to out of a connection to its time and place of origin. And so you regard these objects with considerably more love than you do the chair you sit on every day, or the toothbrush you use in the morning, or the coffee pot you use to brew your coffee. Yes, you could regard these things with equal levels of preciousness, with the same care and attention, and it would not mean that the sentimental object is treated as less. It would mean that your ordinary objects, the things you regard as disposable and replaceable, are actually equally divine, equally precious.

Does this mean you covet them and hold on to them for dear life? No, that is not the relationship of divinity, either. That is attachment and coveting. As those words suggest, you hold on to them as if they were able to ensure your life, your survival, as if having them meant you had a greater claim to existence in this realm. We say this is not true, and that your claim to existence needs no defending, because you do not need any of these things to ensure it. What we mean is that you do not regard these objects as somehow trivial, or as entirely necessary for your survival. You regard them with love, because they showed up in your lifestream at all.

∞

If you are able to treat all objects as equally divine, you should be able to do the same with your relationships. Regard those who enter your lifestream with appreciation for their divinity, rather than engaging with them as a matter of utility, or placing them in a hierarchy of importance.

We would ask that you regard all of your relationships with the same level of divinity—even if they are short-lived, temporary, or not meant to play the same role as each other—because they are still significant, and are still part of your lifestream. And just as you might regard the toothbrush or the seat cushion or any other object that supports you and takes care of you in some manner as part of your physical realm, you might regard all people as part of you, as part of your lifestream, with the same level of regard for their divinity. And then you might see them all differently—not according to the pre-established categories that you use now to evaluate and judge, but with curiosity for how that person entered your lifestream, and for what purpose. How can you honor and acknowledge their divinity in the process?

What do we do with others who do not understand their own divinity and do not regard the divinity of others when they meet them?

That is how they act in separation. How do you relate to them, these pieces of you that are in separation, from you and from others? Can you understand that the impulse to move away is just a narrowing of your world? Can you understand that you are merely fleeing the parts of yourself that are also in separation? You all do this. Meet these parts of you with love. Does that mean you have to agree with their statements, their choices of words, their proclivities and acts? No, of course not. But do not think you can escape separation through separation, by cleaving off parts of yourself that do not fit your idea of a perfect, whole, enlightened being. Yes, those people may be difficult to be around in the sense that they are not sending you love, that they are not recognizing your divinity. But that is where you must meet them: as a source of love and light, as a Seed of Light. Recognize their divinity for them, and in that regard, wake them up. You can be with them and not be in alignment with their behavior or their attitudes. But you do not need to judge them, or move away from them.

But how can I align to people who, for example, only care about winning or losing, without somehow compromising myself?

Your question is how you can relate to each other in regard to winning and losing, and further, whether you can relate to each other through games and sports and activities, where so much judgment and evaluation take place. And we ask you to think about whether you align with winning or losing as a measure of your own self-worth. That is always the case when you are bothered by losing or elated by winning—your sense of self-worth has risen or fallen. That is not a reason *not* to play the game, but it is how you *relate* to the game. Most people cannot relate to winning or losing except as a measure of self-worth. But that does not mean you cannot play the game differently, and enjoy it differently, and relate to all that occurs on the playing field differently.

Aren't games that only serve to divide winners from losers a waste of time?

That is a funny expression: a waste of time. We understand the concern with how time is being spent, or rather, how you devote your energy. Yes, you can decide to put your energies elsewhere and create something. But time is never wasted if you relate to every activity as time in which to know who you truly are. It is true that when you devote time to one activity over another, something else that you wished to do or create will go uncreated—but that is not a waste of time. That is your evaluation of the relative importance of one moment of creation against another, and that is not accurate. Do not evaluate one as more important than another.

The only importance is whether you relate to what is occurring in your life as an expression of love, as an opportunity to know yourself more fully. This is not to ignore the impulse to create something else, and the call to do that, which is what you might really be struggling with. It is not that one activity is a waste, but that another calls, and if you resist, the activity you choose instead *does* become the waste that you see. Simply choose to spend your energy differently; one does not need to evaluate the first as a waste to choose the other.

What about how you choose to spend your time?

Of course, that is a question for many of you: How do you spend your time? A curious phrase—"spend your time." As if it were a monetary exchange with time. You always have the choice of where to align and where to agree, and you can choose a different setting for you and your time. You can choose to express yourself in another place with other people, who can show you who you really are by how you relate to them. But if you choose to go to an event or a venue or some activity, do not judge or denigrate it by virtue of the fact that the people there are not of the vibration that you had hoped to encounter. You must meet them where they are, and honor their divinity, as Seeds of Light. That is all you can do.

And we do not mean to say that you cannot tell someone their behavior is causing harm to others, or that their words contain negative energy. Being with them and meeting them where they are does not mean you must give up any effort to counter their negativity—in the most gentle and affirming way possible. Or, where necessary, with the direct force of a statement that says, no, this is not the way. Yes, you can do that, and still recognize and honor their divinity, for you are saying to another, *You are not recognizing our divinity or your own when you behave this way.* There are circumstances that call for this. But if those people are simply not conforming to the way you would like all beings to be, then you must give up your judgment and try to raise their sense of divinity through your presence, through your love, not through withdrawing yourself and saying, *I can't be bothered with these people.* That is not the way of the Light, and not the path for you, as Seeds of Light, who are meant to show up and illuminate each other's fullness.

We will now focus our teachings on how the Christ Consciousness creates a different way for you to relate to others—for you to break free of the mold your mother and father presented. We will show you all the ways you can redirect and transform relationships in small ways and large, as a reflection of the Christ Consciousness.

22. Releasing Expectation

To move into alignment with the Christ Consciousness means to move out of alignment with the collective consciousness and to break free of your parental archetypes. How can you be in this world and no longer in alignment with it? How do you maintain your relationship with the collective consciousness, which you cannot escape entirely, and still align yourself with the Christ Consciousness? How do you relate to all those who are not in alignment with the Christ Consciousness, but are instead aligned with darkness and negativity? How do you live in alignment with the truth … and still relate to the collective consciousness?

This is the crux of the issue, and we will begin with how you should relate to each other, and to yourselves. We have already said that you all mirror each other and that you must strive to show each other the fullness of what you are. Now, this does not mean you should deny the negative elements that unfold in each and every one of you. We are not asking you to negate anything.

The embodiment of the Christ Consciousness is not a negation. It is not a refusal to look at what you have created and say, *Oh, that was negative, I'll move on.* That is avoidance and a refusal to engage with what you have created.

That is our first lesson: engagement. You must engage with what you have created—and you have created each other. It is as simple as that. You have created each other, and now you must engage with your creation. Do you like what you have created? Does it spread love? Or does it spread hatred and fear? These are the questions you grapple with all the time, and yet your primary mechanism is avoidance. You avoid your own pain, and you do so by avoiding that which you think will *cause* you pain. So you end relationships, and avoid people, and turn away and ignore, in the hopes that the pain will never come to the forefront. And most of the time, it doesn't. It just sits there, waiting to be seen, waiting to be addressed. Because you have given birth to it, created it, and it is therefore part of your consciousness. And you will go on re-creating it again and again as an energetic presence in your life, pushed to the background, constantly avoided, until you face it.

So how do you engage and meet each other, despite all the pain?

You simply *do*. You show up and say, *I am here with you.* That is it. Simply acknowledge, and say, *I am not leaving. I am here with you, and I love you, and I will stay with you.* Start there. Start with expressing the willingness to be with that which you don't want to be with, whether that's a job, a friend, a family member, a situation, an emotion, or anything else. Start with: *I am here with you.* That's it.

It is simple, but that does not make it less profound. It makes it the easiest entry point for any situation. For your first instinct, all of you, is to run the other way, and the second instinct is to argue and control. But when you state something in language, a declaratory statement, you are laying claim to a shared existence. You are laying claim to a relationship, to a connection, and are attesting to the co-creation of two divine beings or Seeds of Light. You are no longer denying your own creation. That is powerful. And you will notice right away how much easier it is to soften and step into the situation simply by saying, *I am here with you*. See the people around you anew in every moment, and see how their constant rebirth shifts everything for you. You need not relate to each other as you have in the past, or even as you did minutes ago. Now you can simply choose to meet the person in the *present* moment, without necessarily imposing the experience of the past onto the present.

∞

We invite you to bring the Christ Consciousness into your relationships with others by *not* assuming that the person is the same as your memory of them. Can you invite in a level of curiosity and wonder about the other person that allows you to honor what they *have* been … and yet hold open a space for something new? Can you regard them in their infinite fullness and capacity for change, so when you see them, you know that at one point they were one type of person—perhaps riddled with anger or suffering from depression or disliking their father or only thinking about money—but might have changed? Can you hold their former self with delicate wonder as you inquire as to who they are now, what they are feeling now, and how they are reacting to all that is unfolding between you? Can you bring the wonder and awe and openness to the possibility that this person is something other than what you expected?

For that is the way of the Christ Consciousness: It sees the other person as an infinite series of possibilities, and sees that you are in co-creation with each other. Allow the past to fall away, no longer a shackle, no longer a requirement. Will you offend someone if you don't remember things about them, or act as if their needs or wishes were not valid? We understand this fear, and applaud the desire to ensure that the other person feels loved and supported. Do not believe that our approach negates that possibility—but work to achieve it through a different means. You can see someone and know they were once in a relationship with drugs and alcohol, or they had an abusive parent, or they lost a very dear friend or a loved one. You can hold on to these things by recognizing they may still be a part of the person's life—without necessarily imposing them as a requirement that they *still* dictate who the person is.

It is the curiosity and wonder that you bring to a relationship which allows that person to be who they are today, rather than performing who they were yesterday or last week for you. What does that look like? For example, if someone you know is a vegetarian, you can ask if they are a vegetarian still—but of course the salience of that question depends on how much time has passed. If it has only been minutes, it's undoubtedly too short a period of time. But if this person was someone you last met six months ago, then it makes sense to want to see if they are still pursuing that particular path of eating. Can you see the difference?

∞

There is no need to relate to each other as if there is a past. You can relate to each other as perfect strangers in the sense of wonder and awe and curiosity that can accompany such relationships. And so you might not assume that someone is fixed or rigid or set in their ways, as you have always assumed in the past. You act with surprise when you see someone and they have changed, or you smile with a kind of ennui when you see someone after some time and they have not changed much at all.

This is unnecessary; you burden them with your past and their past—or more accurately, *your* version of their past, the version that was co-created by the two of you. You have chosen to create your relationships with this other person as they were in the past. Why not co-create a new present, a new moment that does not resemble the past? You can simply invite them in again, anew, with the phrase, *I am here with you now, and I wish to know you now, as you are now, not as I knew you then*. You might ask, *Who is this person? Who is she now?* That is all you have to say and do. Act as if there is more to learn about this person, and wonder who they are now.

That's beautiful.

Yes, so simple, no? We have told you that the ways to relate to each other through the Christ Consciousness are simple. They do not require esoteric or arcane formulas. They do not require the complicated ceremonies or practices that so many of you enjoy and seek, as if complication would allow you to connect more deeply with those around you. It is simple: Stop imposing the past on them. And the past is understood as not only your memories of them, but as the categories of identity and perceptions you take from the collective consciousness, and that shape your impression that, in order to survive, you must treat this person as separate from you. Otherwise, they might kill you or harm you in some way, and threaten your survival.

No, you do not need to bring in the past or the need for survival. And so the formula is simply to say to yourself, *I am with you now, as you are now, not as I once knew you. Who are you today?* And see what type of relationship shows up. See what you can co-create with this person now, without the weight of the past serving as a wedge between you.

∞

We have said that you impose on each other a version of the past as you each remember it, which is never the truth of what occurred. No, that is a past that you have generated, filtered through your own experiences, through your own memory, and therefore, is never truly accurate. By imposing that past on each other, you guarantee you will never escape the confines of the collective consciousness, because you will always be imposing its products, its creations, upon each other, re-creating them again and again, and thus maintaining yourself in alignment with its structures.

By forgiving yourself and others, you release yourself from the past. By saying you are with them here, now, not as they were in the past that you have fabricated, you co-create with them. And now we will speak of the future, of the expectations you place upon each other, which are veiled and very sneaky ways of imposing the past on them. For expectations are future actions that you want to see happen—and those actions are based on past behavior.

Now, expectations are not entirely bad. They do not need to

be a burden. But understand that the way you expect others to behave is often a replica of the past.

Let us make this clear: If you expect and hope and wish for another to have a happier life, to be open to their fullness, that is a wonderful expectation. But we would not even call it an expectation; we would call it a prayer or a wish. It is a request, and you are in alignment with something that is hoping for the higher good of that person. This is something we applaud, because it is an effort to lift someone up and help them see their fullness.

But to expect something of another is to somehow control the outcome of their lives, to demand they undertake certain actions or behave in certain ways that are almost always about protecting you, and are in service to *your* ego. If you expect that someone will do something for you or behave a certain way, you are attempting to anticipate and control the outcome of your mutual co-creation. Your expectation is tied to a fear that they will not behave that way, that somehow your co-creation will take a different form, and this form will be less than the form you expected or would like to see created.

Do you see how much of the collective consciousness has filtered back into your relationship? You are trying to determine that person's existence in time and space from this moment, projected into the future, so that the future moment aligns with *your* binary perception of what is good or better. This is not the way of the Christ Consciousness, for it does not allow for the infinite possibilities that you cannot perceive. And so you expect—which is to say that you limit the possible outcomes.

Can you see the difference between praying for the highest good of all involved, versus praying for the outcome that services you, and only you, even when you think it might be good for the other person, too? Yes, that is the difference. Allow yourself to be in creation with this other person in a way that is open to the possibility of the highest good for you both. You can request, you can pray, and you must then relinquish and let go.

Will the outcome always be for the highest good? No, not necessarily, for that other person is also in a state of expectation about you, and this is often how you co-create—both of you in mutual expectation of how the other person should behave.

How does the Christ Consciousness respond if the other person expects something of us?

You allow them to expect, and you allow whatever will be created between the two of you to unfold, with you holding the hope for the highest good and no expectation—including no expectation that they give up *their* expectations. For that, too, would be to fall into judgment of the other person. Let them expect, and hold their expectation gently. Understand that they are expecting and controlling—it's what all of you do—and see if you can let unfold whatever may be, regardless of the expectation.

It is the alignment with possibility, infinite possibility, that allows for the highest good to emerge. That alignment maintains this space of receptivity and creation. And what unfolds will be different from what would have unfolded had you been in alignment with expectation and control. It may not always look different, but the energy of the experience will be different, for you will be in a space of allowance rather than judgment, rather than comparison with what might have been had the other person behaved as you wished they would.

So when you are with someone, and you are saying to yourself, *I am with you here now, as you are now, not as you were in the past that I created*, then you can ask, with wonder and curiosity, what might emerge between you today. And you allow that to happen, without expectation or demand or effort. Align to the possibility, to the infinite possibilities, and see what happens. That is the way to be with each other in the present, without trying to control the future.

∞

As we previously explained, expectation limits your relationships with each other. Expectation is the demand that the other person become someone that they are currently not—and that they do so for you. So you are asking them to have a future that may not be for their highest good, and may not be what they should do. Of course, it might, and that would be a felicitous outcome, if your expectation and their highest good are aligned. But that does not usually happen. No, what usually happens is that you ask something of someone to ensure your own safety, your own survival, and that is for them to become someone who serves *your* needs. Now, there is nothing wrong if they do so, but their free will ought to lead them to that type of action, not your expectation.

Expectation is also built upon the past—built upon what you think you need, based on your past requirements and experiences. You expect someone to behave in a particular way to justify your understanding of what occurred in the past, and how that shaped your view of reality. You seek confirmation, for in that confirmation you believe you can predict the future—and thereby be prepared for it. It is the same impulse that leads many people to seek out psychics for advice about what will happen in the future. In so doing, they form an expectation of what will occur, so they can help mitigate their feelings of helplessness.

You also impose expectations on how others will behave and feel. You find it disturbing when someone is inconsistent, emotionally, because you cannot predict their moods or what they'll say. You sometimes think that they are "crazy." And yes, there are instances where that behavior is the sign of a mind that is degrading, but that is not always the case. Sometimes people simply surprise you by doing something unexpected, or taking a different approach than you believed they would, based on past experience. And that's just another way in which you're proving that you would like them to conform to a specified outcome, based on your perception of their highest good—and more importantly, *your* highest good.

We understand the desire to do so, but it should not be indulged. Indulging in expectation means you are limiting a person's full expression of divinity, and making a request that they be something other than what they may be intended for at that moment. The vastness of who they *could* be is not something that you can comprehend. No, the range of experiences and the fullness of each person are so vast that you cannot possibly know what is best for the other person. You can only strive to be open to their fullness, to not allow them to limit themselves, and in so doing, pay homage to that fullness. This is your gift to another person—to be able to stand for their fullness, their infinite possibilities of expression, as Seeds of Light co-creating in this realm. When you impose expectations, you limit people by saying that there are possibilities they should not entertain. You reinsert yourself at the core of the relationship as the gravitational pull, and insist this person should orbit you rather than you orbiting each other.

The answer to all of this is very simple: Do not seek to impose, but instead, begin with wonder. *I wonder if so-and-so…* Add to that your wish. And even less demanding would be a formulation like: *I wonder what so-and-so is going to say to me today*, or, *I wonder what so-and-so and I are going to do this weekend.* Be open to the possibilities that this person might show up completely new, having learned something about themselves or about the world, and wanting to share it with you.

∞

How does any of this relate to time, space, and the Christ Consciousness?

You regard each other as separate in time and space. It is an agreement you have come to, before you entered this realm: to experience time and space together, through separation, so that you may come to understand that, at another level, you are not separate at all. You are all energy. And in each moment of the present, in the now, you co-create the experience of separation, again and again and again. That is all there is.

And yet your relationships are structured around time and space in ways that void the present moment, that are merely attempts to co-create in the now versions of the past, and to control the future by demanding and expecting replications of the past. So you always get what you had before. There is a great irony here, in that you are never satisfied. You are always wanting more—something different—and are dissatisfied with what you experience. You do not experience it as the true, unconditional love it is, or realize that, at a quantum level, the life you are experiencing is the purest manifestation of love, and that if you were to be truly present to it, it would overwhelm you with bliss and love. You all have momentary glimpses of this, but the majority of your lives are spent chasing something else.

The irony is that you are dissatisfied because you keep reproducing and demanding the same again, out of fear that you might get something worse. And so when you co-create with each other, you set yourself up to fail by falling into the same trap again and again and again. "More, please" of the reality that doesn't satisfy you. *More!*—again and again. This is what you co-create. It is not a question of blame or fault; it is a question of your mind's effort to protect you from the reality you perceive to be a threat to your existence.

But that is a grand illusion. You cannot be destroyed, and you cannot die. You will only leave your physical form and take on a different one, and be elsewhere, different from what you know now. Yet you think your physical form is the sole vehicle for your life, for your being, and so you replicate the past in order to protect yourself from a future where your physical form might not exist.

This is essentially a way of trying to keep death at bay. The possibility exists, and it is inevitable that you will leave your physical body. You cannot change that. If your form was infinite, you would cease to work through certain issues, and your co-creation in life would stagnate. It is important for you to have a relationship to time and space in this finite form, so that you will work through your karmic issues, even though you are ultimately infinite. And so you spend all of your time and energy—and we mean those words—trying to prevent the one thing you cannot prevent: death. *Just keep it at bay,* you tell yourselves, and so you do. You go through life co-creating with each other in ways that are designed to prevent you from experiencing death, despite the fact that it is one experience of which you can be certain.

Suspend your fear of death and accept that in each exchange there *may* be death. But the real death that you might experience is the death of the ego, in which case you would operate out of wonder rather than expectation, and be filled with the blissful fullness of the possibilities of an exchange, of a co-creation, with every other Seed of Light you come into contact with. You must see where death holds you back—where the fear of annihilation keeps you in check so that you do not express yourself, and do not allow others to express themselves. Instead, you reduce them to categories, to smaller bits of information that you can then evaluate and decipher, to determine how much of a threat to your existence they are. Imagine the types of exchanges you might have—and the lifestreams that might intersect with yours and allow you to see more and more of this glorious realm—if you didn't feel threatened.

Begin to open yourself to the possibility of your own death by allowing the part of you that wants to protect you to let go, slowly, in your interactions with others. Use this simple claim to openness, as we said before: *I wonder...* It will allow you to see what might unfold without control, without expectation. Look for where you are holding onto expectation, even in the slightest way, based on how you perceive another person to be. For when you catch yourself doing that, you can say, *I am here with you now, in the present, as you are now, not as I perceived you to be from the past I have created, and I wonder what you might say to me, what might unfold between us.*

It is that claim to be in the present moment without expectation that gives the other Seed of Light permission to glow and grow in ways you do not anticipate, but might bring you more joy and wonder.

23. Raising Children

How do you remain in the present and avoid replicating the past, including your parental archetypes, when you begin to raise children of your own? Parenting and offspring is a topic that brings up strong feelings for many of you. For children are the primary way in which you impose and replicate the past with each other. As a parent, you come into this world with your views, your language, and your absorption into the collective consciousness.

And when you begin to raise a child, you may wish to raise that child in a way that differs from your own experiences or you parents' experiences. At the same time, you are carrying with you your experiences as a child of a parent, and those experiences infiltrate your own rearing of your child.

This is a source of great pain and consternation for many of you, as you see yourself becoming your parents—or you *resist* becoming your parents—in some way or another. It is inevitable. This is a karmic connection between you, carried over and through into the next generation, and it is laudable to think you might resist or change. But you come to this much too late, after you have already embraced and absorbed those models and patterns, and have not done the work necessary to untangle yourself from those paradigms of behavior. You only notice them as they are emerging in your relationship with your child, and by then they are already a part of your relationship with the child.

So for those who expect to become parents, your role is to work through the paradigms you have inherited from your parents, and from the collective consciousness, so that you may embody a *different* role for your children.

But your children are also a receptacle for your own hopes and dreams, and so not only do you see yourself emulating the past, you draw upon those things in your past that were not realized, or where you believe you made mistakes. And now you wish to save or rescue your child. You hope to avoid in the future a past *you* experienced, and so you think about all the accomplishments that you did not achieve and all that things you regret, and you formulate wishes and prayers for your child for a better life than yours. But this is a form of imposing the past, too. So the way in which you relate to your child is through the effort to control the future by replicating the past. That is, you actively seek to control the outcome in relationship to the past. The past is the dominant touchstone for your entire relationship to the child.

Can you be present, as you are now, with this child? Or do you appear as a collection of ghosts, as a collection of people you no longer experience, in memories and forms that you once remember, now present in a single body?

You are a parade of memories and patterns that you share with the child. How can you be truly present to the child? It is impossible, and that is okay. We only wish for you to see how the mechanism works, without believing that you cannot avoid it altogether. You *cannot* avoid it altogether. It is inevitable, and that, too, is okay. We applaud you for how you raise children and aspire to bring them into a world that is better than the one you have.

But there is a different way, in which you do not have to escape time and space. Instead, you have to learn to *bend* time and space, and relate to time and space in ways that you did not before. This is the beginning of laying down a new path for your child, and for all of humanity. Learning to bend time and space will affect not only how you relate to each other, but how you relate to your children, and how they will relate to *their* children. This is the path of ascension for all of humanity.

24. Bending Time and Space

We are going to explore more deeply what it means to bend time and space, and how to relate to time and space in this way. Then we will show you how to relate to each other according to this new relationship to time and space.

How do you bend time and space? In truth, you all do this all the time already. You just don't realize it, and don't do it consistently. You first began to bend time and space as a child, when you fantasized about life elsewhere. You would vividly imagine other realms and people, and those things would appear to be very real—so real, in fact, that you might see other creatures or have imaginary friends, or a life that seemed so powerful you would be distracted for hours, playing in it. You lost all sense of time, and fell *out* of time, because your creative faculties were so engaged that you were in fact in another time and place rather than *this* time and space, where everything continued to operate according to collective agreement. So you first began to experiment with time and space by leaving this place's clock and escaping the agreement of the collective consciousness. And so time would "fly." Yes, that is your expression; time would move quickly, and you would stop experiencing it.

Your perception of time is based on your ability to experience it and be aware of it. Time will speed up when you are no longer aware of it, and you are no longer aware of it when you are immersed in the field of space that you occupy. As a child, this was a space of fantasy, as you called your other realms through your creative faculties. And you experienced the time in *those* realms, unaware of the passage of time in *this* realm. And this continued as you began to play with other children. You would still lose time, and you would imagine other roles for yourselves, and perhaps imagined you were in other locations, this time with other children rather than on your own. You would craft something with others, like being in an adventure together in some other realm, and this would be your governing relationship to space. You would adapt your surroundings to that space, by modifying it or just building it with your imagination. And so this was your relationship to space. You would reimagine the world around you and relate to space in that way.

As a child you learned to relate to time and space by bending it, by allowing a portion of yourself to escape the time and space of the collective consciousness, of this earthly realm. You were able to experience it differently, through another realm of your own creation. But this does not mean you left time and space altogether. No, you could not. This is not the way, because you were already immersed and almost entirely absorbed by the collective consciousness. And so while you could exit it as part of your perception, you were still a part of it when your mother called you back to the house if playtime was over.

∞

Bending time and space requires you to be entirely present to the moment, so you can see that the moment does not exist—not as you think it does. And that is the key: *not as you think it does*. It is a moment that can be experienced, but the minute you are thinking about it, you are already out of it; you have fallen away from the experience and removed yourself from the purity of it. You are now filtering it through your mind.

That is normal, and is how you all do it, but bending time and space requires you to do things differently—to be in the now in a way you very rarely are. To do so successfully means that you experience time and space bending, but are not *thinking* about bending time or space. This is the crux of the example of your childhood experience in creative visualization, where you imagined yourself to be elsewhere, and then lost track of time and space as the agreement of this realm. So in the now of your creation, you were no longer aware of the time that occurred in your reality. You bent time, so that time may have appeared to go by very quickly. When you reconnected with this time, this realm, much time had passed, and yet you may have felt like you were in that other realm for only a moment. You do the same in dreams, at night while asleep, and occasionally when daydreaming. This, too, is quite normal.

Are we only talking about speeding up our perception of time by being aware of it? Is that not being out of the now?

For now, understand that this is only one way to bend time. The key to your question is to understand that because there is no time, really, there are in fact infinite strands of time. Just as there are many universes that might exist, so, too, are there many times. This is the reality that you experience all the time without realizing it: There are realms of life occurring all around you of which you are not aware, each of which is independent and yet entirely connected. You are not aware of all the microbes and whatnot occurring at certain physical levels, nor of all the energetic shifts around you, nor even of the spiritual realms that envelop you—those Light Beings you call *ghosts* or *spirits*, which permeate your life without you being conscious of them. And those all operate with a different sense of time, a different relationship to the linear expression of objects in some form of separation from each other. So bending time and space is not something you do to time as much as it is allowing yourself to merge with and experience another realm of time. It is to step out of time, into another wavelength or frequency, so that your experience of time changes.

But that does not mean you escape time entirely. As we have said, you must experience time as part of your evolution, your ability to understand and work with energy. Time is an essential element of this process, even if at a quantum level there is no time. Time is the gift of consciousness so that you can experience yourself in separation and come to know what it means to be divine. Time is the portal that allows you to accomplish this, to undertake this experience, and therefore, you cannot escape it altogether. But you can "bend" it by stepping into and aligning with other dimensions that surround you.

This is, in fact, what you do when you daydream or imagine another world as a child. You lose track of this time as an element of consciousness, as perception. And so we can tell you that expanding your perception of time in this realm involves deepening your relationship to it—to be truly in the now in this realm—so that you can be aware of each moment without being aligned in another dimension. That is what happens when you meditate and become acutely aware of your body and its sensations, the temperature in the room, little sounds and smells, and aches and pains. Suddenly, everything that you normally filter out comes rushing in, and you are aware of so much data, so much sensation, so much perception of the present moment that you do not usually permit yourself to experience. And the mind does not want to experience this. It finds it overwhelming—after all, it has been filtering it out for years—and now finds it too much. So the mind gets annoyed or bored or angry. And you find the experience of time becomes excruciating. Each second expands beyond what you could have imagined, feeling like an eternity.

And this is the perception of time as you come to feel time's fullness, the fullness of each moment, with all of the life that is teeming in that second, and life meaning everything—all of the sounds, sensations, and experiences that you suddenly become aware of filling that moment. It is this fullness that you begin to experience for the first time as you slow down, as the mind slows down and ceases to filter out certain data. That sudden awareness of fullness, the fullness of life in each second, means you begin to perceive each second as being slower. You slow down and begin to account for all of this other data.

This is the bending of time, and you can relate to this moment, and time, as an agreement of the collective consciousness in this realm, by experiencing it fully, by allowing for the effulgence of it all to penetrate you, often for the first time. Initially, yes, each second can be boring, can be overwhelming, as the mind, so accustomed to filtering and pushing away so much of reality, begins to experience it—to deeply and profoundly experience reality in each second, just as it is. We promise you that over time, you will come to experience this fullness not as excruciating boredom or like time is standing still, but as utter bliss, as you embrace this fullness and equate it with what it really is: love. The fullness of each second, all of the life it contains, is but an expression of divine love, and you are slowly becoming aware of that fullness, of how deep that love is, by slowing your mind and thereby bending time and space in a manner that slows down the mind so it takes in a great deal more than you are used to experiencing in a single moment.

∞

We want to continue to deepen your understanding of what it means to bend time and space, and this bending is not, as we said, a manipulation of time in the way you might think, like you exercising control over time or others, or stopping time with some sort of magic amulet. No, we speak of bending time and space in regard to you moving into and out of alignment with time as you know it—the time that you all agreed to as part of your incarnation in this realm. You move out of alignment with this time, partially, at least for a while, until you are able to move back into alignment with it, and what you are doing during that period is aligning yourself with another aspect of creation, another frequency, another dimension that coexists with this one. You did this as a child and you can do it even now, as you move into and out of alignment with the present moment. And we explained that the present moment is a place where you can align and truly slow down so that you can feel the fullness of this second in this realm.

How do you align to other frequencies? Can you speed up the present moment in this realm? You must understand that you never escape this realm of time entirely. You cannot, for the simple reason that your body and mind are still partly in it. For how else have you lived your life but as incarnated in this physical realm? So even as you might travel in consciousness, your body is still in this physical realm. It has not left, and parts of you still remain aware of and connected to this realm, and so you are still bound to time as it exists here.

That is why you cannot escape aging through mind travel. You will still age, your body will still move through time and space, and you will grow older. And it is this notion of death that is at the core of so many of your relationships, and we wish to emphasize this so that you understand that your primary relationship with all things, all people, all of creation, really, is built around your fear of this inevitability. Yes, your physical form will perish. Bending time and space has nothing to do with avoiding death. We do not wish you to approach this with the view that you can transcend physical life simply by willing your consciousness to align with another life, another realm. Yes, it is true that you can lengthen and extend your life in a physical body, because as you heal yourself, heal your relationships, and heal your relationship with the inevitability of death, then the negative energy, fear, and anger that you carry with you, particularly around death, will no longer be reproduced. You will co-create yourself in and through other Seeds of Light without those fears, and that will allow you to expand your ability to live in this physical realm.

∞

How do you align yourself with other realms? It is the same thing you did when you were a child. You align yourself emotionally, mentally, and physically. Did you recognize what you were doing as a child, as you became completely absorbed in that imaginary, fantasy realm? Yes, you were absorbed, and we have used that word to describe your attachment to the collective consciousness of this realm, and how you can become equally absorbed in another realm. You do not have to accept reality as it appears to you, or as it is described to you in words. The physical reality that you have all agreed to and many are aligned with is actually an illusion that you have all created together. That does not mean it's like an image on TV. There is a difference, for example, between watching a TV actor die on screen and a person die in real life. But you might think of the collective consciousness as a large human TV network, which you have all created together, out of the infinite energy that you all are. You have chosen the channels, and you are now watching this season's episodes play out, wondering, *Why are we experiencing the same narrative again and again?* Well, why not change the channel?

You can change the channel, and that is what you do when you bend time and space through creative visualization. Just as you did when you were a child, you can imagine other forms of life, other ways of being, other relationships, other connections, all in the mind's eye, through your creative faculties. And this is just the beginning of aligning with another realm. You bend time and space by allowing yourself to experience it. Some of you call this daydreaming or flights of imagination, and there's a hint of disparagement, as if you were not doing anything "real" when you did it. And it is true that some of you do it to escape reality—to avoid your connection to the collective consciousness—and this is just another form of escaping the fear of death. When reality in the form of the collective consciousness is too much for you, you flee to an imaginary realm instead of grappling. Your motive for aligning with a new realm is fear-based, because you are afraid that reality as it currently exists is not enough, or that you do not belong in this realm, that you are not loved here. And so you flee to another realm.

That is not the ultimate reason for aligning with another realm, for bending time and space. No, the reason to align this realm with another is to draw them closer in frequency, so that you might bridge the gap between that realm and this one. When you're doing this, do not imagine a fantastic, imaginary realm of magic and play. No—imagine a realm just like this one, but one that lacks negativity and is full of Light. Begin to imagine this world differently. Do not flee it. Be in it, but be in it and in alignment with a higher version of it—a version of it where love flows more freely. And in so doing, you will bring that realm into this one.

You are bending time and space through your alignment with the energy of the other realm, not through the manual creation of this realm. The problem is that when you try to "fix" this realm the way you do via normal means, you end up replicating what was already here in a different form, in a new way. This is why your images of other magical realms always end up resembling this realm, at the level of content and structure—just lots of greed and anger and war, and all those human dramas. And this is what you do when you flee to another realm: You actually end up transporting this realm with you to that other realm. So no, the answer is not to create a magical realm where you can play, which is what you already do with TV and movies. Instead, imagine this realm differently and act in alignment with that new vision, with that new realm.

How do we stop replicating the same structures and paradigms in our world?

Part of the answer is that you must do the internal work of becoming aligned with the Christ Consciousness and imagining life from there. How do you align with the Christ Consciousness as the vehicle for accessing another realm? For many of you could very well dream up realities and other fantasy worlds that resemble this one in structure, much as you do with most of your television and fiction. But those stories are merely the same narrative of the ego and separation written again and again, with different characters, and creative elements like magic. And you see the same plot lines played out until you tire and need something more.

No, the Christ Consciousness is the vehicle through which you align with a new reality, to shape time and space in that manner. It is the vehicle that says there is no time, there is no separation, and you can only access the present moment. Otherwise you are simply recreating versions of the past. So how do you align with and therefore co-create a new reality, one that is built on the Christ Consciousness and not on separation?

It is a slow process—ironic, given all of our emphasis on time—and yes, it is slow insofar as it is measured against time that appears in the collective consciousness, as part of that agreement for experiencing reality. When you recognize that this is a process by which the collective consciousness is undergoing its own alignment, you can see that what is happening is that, at each moment, the collective consciousness aligns with a slightly different frequency, a different vibration. Or, more accurately, it is re-created anew as a different frequency. That is what you are all capable of doing.

What can you do personally to align to a different reality? You can see that there is no past, there is no tie to the past, and there is nothing that requires you to re-create yourself in this moment as what you once were. You can therefore release and re-create yourself anew, to resurrect yourself as pure, whole, and without trauma. You are capable of this, and you can do it, as we have explained, through forgiveness, which allows you to re-create yourself without the burdens of wrongdoing that you attribute to yourself and others.

Can you imagine a world where you love rather than hate? Can you imagine a world where you are not separate from others? That is the key; as you deepen your connection to the Christ Consciousness, as you learn to forgive and rebirth yourself instantaneously, you will see you are not different, that all of your ways of dividing up the world do not matter, and are simply the products of a mind, an ego, built around separation. And so you can align to the possibility that people will not hold themselves apart from each other in the same ways as they have in the past. They will no longer hold tight to the structures of identity that they believe must exist in order for them to be seen, in order for them to have a foothold in this realm, and to lay claim to their existence. You can begin to imagine, to call forth, through your own creative visualization, a world in which someone, anyone, believes they belong by virtue of being alive and here, in a human body—not because they have laid claim to exist in any particular way.

There is nothing about that that will achieve ultimate emancipation. As we have explained, these are all necessary effects of separation; a response to the claim that you are not worthy or that you do not belong or that your identity is flawed. Imagine, again and again, as you approach people in your lives, that they are shedding their identities, that they are looking past the separation and seeing each other as divine creations, Seeds of Light, equal in the eyes of God, all deserving of complete abundance. Imagine them co-creating each other anew, as perfect beings, in their fullness, the fullness of their soul's expression, as those who they were meant to be, and without the prejudices and burdens of the past. There is no need for judgment, no need for penance. You can re-create yourself anew now.

And what about those who have been marginalized and discriminated against in the past? How will they be treated in this process? For now, understand that the process is one of co-creation, and in this vibration, you will enter into relationships with others without the burden of the past and the expectations of who they might be. You meet them where they are, and at the same time, imagine them aligning with a new reality, where they can co-create themselves without the burden of the past, without the fear and negativity. And they, in turn, can begin to forgive themselves and others completely. As a result, they can align with a different realm as well, where peace and abundance flow easily.

That is your mission now: to bend time and space in and through your relationships, with all people. Bending time and space means to meet others where they are, to see them in the present moment—not as you wish they would be, but as they *are*. Simultaneously, begin to align yourself with a new reality, where they, too, are in alignment with their highest self. Can you maintain this dual perspective? Can you avoid the pitfall of judging someone for not being where you want them to be, of wishing they were different, of criticizing them for not being emancipated or enlightened, and actually holding the resonant space for them to align with that higher version of themselves? This is the difference. The first is a place of judgment, where you stand and compare them to what they might be, or what you think they should be, and the other is an intention, and a feeling—a place of energy where you stand and hold a place of love so that they might be their higher self, whatever that looks like. For you do not know exactly who they are meant to be in their full expression. That is the difference.

You can bend time and space by being in the fullness of the moment with each person and aligning to the highest possibility: *I am here with you now, as you are, not as I wish you would be, and I am aligned to the highest good for all involved.* You can meet them in the present from a place of fullness, of your own fullness, so that they may be drawn, in their own way, on their own volition, to that higher frequency. That is done not through cajoling or explaining or prodding, but through presence, through the fullness of your own Seed of Light shining brightly in and through your physical form, and reaching them in ways that are beyond the mind and beyond comprehension.

25. Forgiving Our Parents

As you can see, you can relate to each other in time and space and through the Christ Consciousness, and bend time and space in order to align with a different way of being. You can speed up your experience of the present moment by aligning with a different realm, or slow down your experience by aligning with this realm and feeling the fullness of each second. You can meet people where they are, and in this way, align them to another possibility—one that allows them to meet you there, but does not use words to cajole or push them to be something other than they are now.

You all have difficulty with aligning with another reality, because you are consistently aligning with the collective consciousness—

specifically with aspects of your mother and father figures. It is about the relationship you had to these two archetypes, to these two ways of relating to energy. Don't you find it odd how little the figures of the mother and father have changed, though what you think a man can be and what a woman can be *have* changed? Don't you find it ironic that despite all your efforts to break out of a mold of binary genders, you necessarily gravitate toward these two roles when you're relating to your children or to each other? These are the primal models that you all inherit. Whether you are with one mother and one father or two mothers or two fathers, it does not matter. In some way you will absorb from them their relationships to mothers and fathers, and take on those relationships. It is the way it has been, and so it is now. That is not the way it will always be, and that is why we are here now, but if you do not realize that you *need not* replicate those models, you, too, will end up doing the same thing your fellow human beings have done for millennia.

So how do you relate to the mother and father differently, so that you do not replicate them? And how does this relate to bending space and time?

It is because of your difficulties with the parental figures, which become the paradigm for nearly all of your relationships with the rest of the world, that you have difficulty aligning with another frequency or realm. You find it hard to bend time and space in a way that allows for you to accelerate your growth. Instead, you find yourself slipping into old patterns, or you suddenly see some aspect of yourself, and think, *I'm becoming my mother*. Or you realize that you've never really forgiven your father. And those things play out in so many other areas of your life. You align once again to a reality shaped by the past and that you project onto the future, and you might think in your saddest moments that there is no other way.

We are here to say that is not true; there is another way, there is the way of the Christ Consciousness, and so we begin by asking you to forgive your parents. Truly forgive them. For they were the products of *their* parents, and the collective consciousness as they were absorbed by it, and so on and so forth, in the past, for generations and generations. This is your lineage, and you have inherited that karma. You will find that the energy of that karma continues with you, because you have learned patterns from them, and so you replicate them.

So forgive your parents regularly for all that they have given you, even though you may not want it. It is yours. It was gifted to you when you incarnated in that lineage, so please accept your gift.

Now, how do you relate to the father and mother figures in a way that is liberating and does not require you to feel beholden to the past? Once you have forgiven them, simply see yourself in the present, and accept that there are aspects to your personality, patterns and tendencies, that you associate with your parents. And just accept them. That is the first step. You cannot actually erase them or stop reproducing them without first accepting them. And once you have accepted them, you can align to the possibility that you are no longer producing them. This is already happening when you forgive, because when you forgive, you erase the past. You revise your present experience of the past by rewriting the past, by saying that the wrong you perceive now in the present did not occur, that there was never any wrongdoing. And so there is no wrongdoing in the past, nor in the present, nor will there be in the future. This is the power of the resurrection—to resurrect yourself in the present moment, without the burden of the past.

And so you forgive your parents and ask yourself, *What would it be like to react to the world separate from my parents' reactions?* You can wonder what it would be like to embrace the world in a different way—a way not shaped by your parents' patterns. Just posing the question already begins to align you to another possibility. But notice that you are not doing it to get away from your parents. You've forgiven them and accepted that this is how you've done things in the past, and decided that now you wish to try something different. See what it feels like, and what happens. There is no judgment of what you've been. You're simply opening up the possibilities of how and who you *can* be by realizing that you do not need to become your parents. There is no requirement. Nothing about your birth requires you to embrace and accept those patterns and traits that you learned from your parents.

Is it really that simple?

It is that simple. We did not say it was easy. It is not easy, for you have inherited patterns that have persisted for ages and generations, and you've spent the better part of your life embracing and absorbing them. To be able to accept those aspects of yourself from your parents—and then choose a different path—requires you to slowly stop reproducing yourself in their image, and to recreate yourself anew. Then you can choose other aspects of yourself for expression, and you can align to the possibility that you can be more than what you believed, based on those two templates. Your mind may resist, because it has known itself as such, and this is what we've described: The mind has to catch up to the energetic changes that occur in all of the subtle bodies and energy fields and chakras.

∞

We now wish to expand this teaching by deepening what it means to be a father and a mother, for we have already touched on the archetypal figures. You treat mothers as these creatures of compassion and unconditional love, always defending their children, so that they become the emotional support system. You regard the father as the sustainer and supporter through physical means; the father who manifests and provides the physical or material support in this realm, and for whom emotional connection may be difficult. These are your archetypes.

Of course these are only archetypes, and you have many different types of parents, and many ways in which parents do not live up to these models, or take different approaches. As archetypes, each of them is a model that provides a means for how you relate to ego separation. For the father views the world as a place in which a certain a type of power and domination must exist, as certain authority over other objects and people, in time and space, in order to ensure survival. The father archetype is therefore the creator in the sense of manifesting physical reality, or generating an exchange and earning money for the labor that is produced. He provides a necessary bulwark against the passions that would ostensibly undermine one's ability to obtain that physical or material support. Mothers, on the other hand, are expected to provide and nurture, taking what the father gives and transforming it into the sustenance for emotional support and well-being of the children.

These are generalities, and the simplification of these figures does not mean we are not in full command of our knowledge of what the mother and father are, or how gender works in your realm. You make gender much more complicated than is necessary.

So we ask you to see where the father and mother figures appeared in your life, and how you related to those figures as children, to see what models and patterns you learned. In what ways did you learn to relate to emotions through your father or mother? In what ways did you react to the world according to your father's views, and in what ways did you absorb your mother's views? For many of you, nearly all of you, will go in search of love from the father in certain areas of your life, and in search of the love of the mother in other areas of your life. This is the way in which those patterns infiltrate and permeate your life's relationships, and your relationships with others.

Let's say, for instance, that your father was someone who was a bit abusive and would often yell, and would tend to get upset if your mother challenged his authority in any way. Perhaps not to the point of physical abuse, but through a threatening pose, or maybe even by storming out of the house or grabbing her arm while in conversation. As a child, you may have been alarmed by this behavior. You may have found it difficult to understand, and you may have experienced only anger and rage at your father. But perhaps he did not feel that life served him well, or thought he hadn't gotten his just rewards, or that he was somehow cheated. And being angry and trying to control your mother became an outlet.

You will no doubt have absorbed a certain amount of this tendency, and it may manifest in ways you could not have anticipated. Not as an exact replica of your father. You may, for example, have become very disciplined and hard-working, and find yourself often quite angry at others who don't seem to put in as much effort—especially if they still do well or even better than you. Or perhaps you get very angry at yourself for not being enough. Perhaps you absorbed a sense of anger about the world not being fair, and think your only way to counteract that is to assert control over your own behavior, by becoming disciplined and working very hard. You have internalized your father's voice as your own internal commander, to ensure that you will not fall to the same fate. Yet you still resent those who manage to do well without your sense of work or dedication, and again, the world is somehow unfair because those who got by with privilege or other means are still rewarded, and you, who worked hard—unlike your father—still find yourself battling to get ahead.

This is but one example of how the father figure establishes your relationship to the world at large, and this will have affected your relationships with coworkers, fellow students, teachers, etc., as you went through life, trying to ensure that you achieved a certain success which eluded your father.

We repeat: There is nothing wrong with this. This is what happens to you, but you must forgive your father for instilling it in you. It was not his "fault"; it was not done with the intent to harm you. No, this is the byproduct of a parent who passed along energetic patterns, or karma, to their children, and it is up to the child to determine what form they take and how they emerge. And so you will replicate these patterns again and again throughout your lifetime. By forgiving your father and accepting this aspect of yourself, you can make conscious choices to re-create yourself in your own fullness, differently.

Doesn't this sound like psychotherapy?

Yes, it might, but most psychologists only help you to explain why your mind processed material in a certain way, what stories you generated as a child to understand the world around you, and how this led to certain patterns. But you do not need to unwind the story. You do not need to go to a therapist to unravel the past, although doing so can be a good thing. Just understand that there is a means of escaping this pattern by forgiving that parent for their role in it, and choosing, consciously, a new way of being.

How does all of this relate to judgment and compassion?

It is precisely the acceptance we speak of that encompasses judgment and compassion. For when you recognize you are judging your parents for all their wrongdoings and misgivings, and then embrace those same traits, you end up judging and condemning them and then doing the same thing to yourself. You look at your parents and identify traits you do not agree with, and then you find that you embody them, too, and you revile yourself in much the same way that you reviled *them*. So the act of co-creating yourself in and through another, or with them, requires that you first let go of that judgment, and simply accept it for what it is: a byproduct of the collective consciousness. And give them compassion for the fact that they did not have the tools or guidance to be able to align with a different way of being—that they were absorbed into the collective consciousness and received patterns from *their* parents, who received them from *their* parents, and that this lineage karma affects them all. That is all you must do—accept it, and you are already bringing the light of compassion to those relationships.

That is the starting point of healing: accepting those things that you resist and revile. By doing so, you begin to heal those relationships, which are splintered and fractured.

But it is with the archetypes that we wish to spend some time, for the archetypes you have learned—the traits you have associated with the figures of the mother and the father—are not necessarily what you need to *understand* those figures. The father and mother figures represent modalities for relating to the world, and now we wish to connect this concept with the act of forgiving and the Christ Consciousness.

To sanctify, as we previously explained, means to honor and express its wholeness, the wholeness of what is. It is to express that wholeness through its recognition. And to sanctify is what the father and mother figures, in their divine forms, are meant to do for you. They operate differently, and this is not, to be sure, a genetic or biological distinction. We are speaking here of the roles that the father and mother figures play in bringing about the realm of separation, and then merging again with and through the Christ Consciousness. In their purest form, the mother and father figures teach you to relate to the physical realm in and through different modalities.

Let us say there is a role for the person who provides raw material, who provides the core substance, and there is another role for the person who manipulates and shapes it into different forms. You might say the first is a producer, the other an engineer, or the first a generator and the other a craftsman. In other words, there is a separation between the creation of the material and the form that it takes. Now, that is ultimately a distinction that does not hold. For as we have said, there is no time and space, and everything is formed in an instant, at each instant, again and again and again. There is no difference really between the substance from which something is made and the form it takes. But you can also hold onto this distinction, when we say that everything is energy, and yet it does take a form—the chair, the desk, the house, the car, the person, etc. In other words, the raw material is one aspect of creation, and the specific form it takes is another. The entire universe is made up of love, of the energy of unconditional love, but the specific forms it takes are infinite, and you can see all of them as both forms and as energy all at the same time.

But it is important to understand that you experience the physical realm as such; that there is raw material and it takes different shapes and forms, and the raw material itself is not the same as the form it takes. So there is nature, which partakes of the earth, and there are plants and animals, and there is the wind, and the sun, and the water, and you are all interconnected—but you are not the same form. There is an important relationship between these two modalities, and that is the entry point for rethinking your relationships, and how you relate to those two modes.

For now, we will close with this idea of these two ways of relating to the physical realm, to separation, and how you see form as being made up of all the same substance, or different substances that themselves take different forms. It's all energy, it's all love, but then it's also separate—human, animal, nature, etc.

26. Beyond Form

Both masculine and feminine modalities are associated with the creation of form, and therefore to form itself. Or, to put it differently, the basic building blocks or elementary material, and the shaping of that material into form.

What are those, and why do they matter? This seems to be a departure from ways of relating to other people.

We assure you they are not, for these principles inform how you relate to all that is. So let us begin by pointing out that form and substance are, respectively, the masculine and feminine principles. The raw material is the feminine principle, and the changing of that raw material into form is the masculine principle. We will return to how these principles relate to your human form, but for now understand that all form is made up of the same building blocks, but takes different shapes. There is the universal force: *shakti*, unconditional love, *chi*, whatever you want to call it—the energy that is at the core of everything, and that is the basic, fundamental building block of all of creation. And then there is the principle that shapes this into numerous forms.

The first is the feminine principle, the base material from which everything comes, while the masculine principle is the creation or shaping of that material into other forms. And you might think of this in terms of Divine Mother and Divine Father—the Divine Mother is the *shakti*, the universal energy or unconditional love that flows through all of the universe; the Divine Father is the principle that shapes that energy into different forms, creating the multitude of forms that this energy can take. That is all that is really meant by these two poles. And, in fact, you need not call them Divine Mother or Divine Father at all, but they are connected to how you relate to the masculine and feminine principles, and so we do not wish to ignore that connection.

It is important to understand that you relate to these aspects of life—energy and form—very differently, and you often do not understand *how* you relate to them. That is how and why you relate to people differently. To put it one way, you know that you are all born from the same energy, and yet you take many forms. And these forms are the things that you end up privileging, over the universal energy that you all are. This is the start of your discrimination and differentiation, and how you privilege some forms over others. And this means that, in a sense, you are privileging the Divine Masculine over the Divine Feminine. That is, you privilege the form over the shared content or substance that gave rise to that form. This is not a mistake of the Divine Father; this is the mistake of your ego and your perception based on how the collective consciousness tells you to view the world.

And that is why we are entering the era of the Divine Mother, where you see the shared underlying stratum of energy that makes up all of life. This is what it means to become aligned with the feminine principle. And it becomes the basis for the way you relate to each other as the same, as equals. The creative force of the Divine Father, of the masculine principle, generates all of the possible forms out of that energy, and it is a wondrous creation, to see that life takes so many forms.

But, from the perspective of the collective consciousness, you do not see that creation as just one expression of the same divine energy—the Divine Mother's *shakti* or power. Instead, you see one form as being different from another form, and disregard that they are built from the same energy—and this means you do not treat all forms equally. You privilege form over the substance from which the form took shape.

We are entering the realm where you can look beyond form, beyond the ways you have privileged form, and the masculine principle, to see the divine energy, the Divine Mother's power, at work in all things. We are entering the realm of the Divine Mother, where the feminine principle—which is simply that all are equal, because you are all born from the same energy—will take root.

How does this affect relationships? This is the principle that says you are all equal. But because you didn't see the world in that way, most of your actions have been in alignment with the Divine

Masculine—with the privileging of form—rather than with the Divine Feminine—with the privileging of the underlying energy you all share.

This has affected your relationships with each other. And this is connected to how you view gender. You have traditionally aligned such behavior, and attitudes of aggression, physical violence, anger, or power, with the masculine, and have associated tenderness, love, and compassion with the female form. This is not an alignment that is required or essential. There is nothing about life, its survival, or its expansion that requires this alignment. But you have done so, and that is part of the reason your collective consciousness has for so long privileged the male form at the expense of the female form, subjugating the feminine to the masculine. The collective consciousness views these two forms not as two perfect creations made by the Divine Father from the Divine Mother's energy, not as two different manifestations of the same energy, but as two different forms that must have two different sets of characteristics, and in which one is placed in a hierarchical relationship to the other.

So that is the key for you: to understand that you often associate certain types of characteristics with one form over another, and fail to see that none of this is required. This is all a product of the collective consciousness that has managed separation by privileging the manifestations of the Divine Father at the expense of the Divine Mother.

∞

Now we will seek to answer the question of how this relates practically to your relationships. The answer is rather straightforward, and that is that you are learning to release your attachment to form, and to see the underlying shared energy of creation that has given rise to that form. You are no longer worried about it as a surface phenomenon, as something to behold and evaluate and judge. This is the collective consciousness at work. Instead, you are learning to realize that it is all born of the same energy, and is all the same at the level of creation. It is all energy and love, and nothing more. And the idea that it takes different forms is the masculine principle, while the idea that it comes from the same source is the feminine principle. As we enter the feminine age, as we leave behind this masculine age, we will no longer privilege one form over another, but recognize the infinite possibilities of all forms being derived from a single source. Isn't that amazing? Can you celebrate the multiplicity of forms by seeing how creative it can be to come from something like love, or energy, all of it giving rise to such variety, such diversity?

This is what life is about: the constant proliferation of love into more and more forms. So you no longer need to look at a form and wonder if it's better or worse or whether it threatens you or not. You can instead revel in its uniqueness, in the fact that it is one form that came from the same source, and revel in the fact that the source of creation can produce so much, so many different types of people and animals. Life takes so many forms, and yet you see and privilege only a few. Instead of worrying about whether someone before you is one form or another, can you simply see that person as a Seed of Light, as the divine manifestation that they are?

You can now see how your masculine tendencies, which are rooted in the need for survival, and fear of death and separation from all others, take over and draw distinctions and try to manage difference so that you are not lost or threatened. None of that is necessary when you are in concert with all of it as just one more manifestation of life. Do you see how you can dissolve your own difference by seeing the other person and you as cosmic family, as the emanation of the same energy from the same source?

There is great beauty and liberation in being able to dispense with external form as the means by which you evaluate and measure the relative value of another person, and instead revel in their uniqueness, in their version of Light. This allows you to shed the fear that you are somehow threatened, that you are somehow not seen or less valuable, and therefore need to fight for your form to maintain your foothold in this realm. You can see yourself, too, as a Seed of Light, as a manifestation of God in just one unique form. See the beauty in yourself, for your uniqueness is also a manifestation of the Divine. That is what is meant by the simple phrase, *namaste*, which many of you have embraced. But you can see it as true—that you can recognize the Divine in you and the other person. That is what you share by virtue of being alive. That is all you really need to know. The person before you stands as a living testament to the power of creation. What else is there to know?

∞

When you recognize the other person's divinity and see their fullness, their true self, beyond form, and allow this person to see your fullness, your divinity, beyond form, you allow each other to shine a little brighter. Then you can align yourself to an even higher frequency, and each of you will allow yourself to align a bit higher, a bit higher, a bit higher, each time. This is the bending of time and space, for you allow each other to align to a version of reality that is not fully anchored here, that is not yet manifest, but is a possibility and can be called into form, into being, here in this realm. Can you see the other person in their highest form? Can you allow that person to come through? Can you invite that person? Yes, you can. You can do so by laying claim to their divinity, and saying, *I stand before you, with you, as you are now, bearing witness to your fullness, to the highest version of yourself.* And that is all you need to do. To be present to the highest version of them as they stand before you.

Isn't this a contradiction from what you said before, about being with you as you are, not as I want you to be?

There is no contradiction. The difference, of course, is that you cannot determine for yourself what that person's highest self is. All you can do is witness it, invite it to appear, and be open to how it manifests. The other way is you imposing on each other versions of what you think each person should be, which often does not reflect their highest selves, but rather your view of what's best. And your view of what's best for another person is often too partial, too limited. So you relinquish the claim to control the other person, and open yourself to the experience of that person as a higher version of their true self. That is the alignment you bring forth when you stand before them in that way. And this is the way in which you co-create each other differently, beyond the collective consciousness, beyond the time and space to which you have agreed as part of the collective consciousness. This is co-creation through the Christ Consciousness.

∞

It is important for us to emphasize that we are not saying that the masculine and feminine principles, which we could give another name, have anything to do with men and women in any real way. That is the way you have all come to create those categories, and how you have shaped your views of what men and women can be, and that is why we use those terms. They help you see the ways you have pigeonholed men and women into certain categories: Men embrace the masculine impulse to shape and create form, and women embrace the impulse to provide the source for creation, to provide the energy that gives rise to creation. This is, again, not essential to either gender. This is your construct of the two genders.

As you relate to the masculine and feminine impulses in your lives, ask yourself: Where do you strive to create? Where do you hold a place of love? Where do you seek to empower yourself? Where do you have compassion and empathy for others? Because you have aligned these questions with gender in your realm, and so you will inevitably associate them with your parental figures. For example, a child might relate to creativity and the impulse to shape oneself through how the father has embodied that masculine impulse. Perhaps your father was not particularly good at creation, did not work very hard, was not ambitious, or chose to live a life of very low expectations—however you might characterize it. And so your relationship to the idea of how you become you will in fact be related to your relationship to your father.

Similarly, you may not have felt very loved, or that your mother was unable to provide you with love and comfort and support, and so you will relate to the issues of love and support, both giving and receiving, through your relationship with your mother. This is how you will replay those relationships in your dealings with other people. These principles or impulses get infused into the dynamics you and your parents set within you, as you co-created each other and become inculcated in the values of the collective consciousness. And then you will impose those dynamics on relationships with the world, co-creating others that match those dynamics.

The impulses of form and energy—the source of energy and what you choose to create from it—form a matrix that you have received from your parental figures. This matrix, steeped in the collective consciousness, dictates how you relate to the energy that lies within all of creation, and the specific form that it takes. And so you must develop an awareness of what your parents taught you and how that is linked to the relationship you share with those parents, for that is how you relate to these impulses in your life.

This is the unraveling of karma you must undertake as you step into alignment with the Christ Consciousness, because that is how you bring the past into the present, and thus into the future. You do so through these matrices, as you co-create. For what we are speaking of now is the matrix of co-creation. We have spoken of how you co-create the world around you in each instant, and how the past becomes the present and the future, and so you are never really in the present, but are always re-creating the past to anticipate the future. And now we are focusing on the matrices you use to generate that world. And this is the twin impulse of energy consolidated into form, the feminine and masculine impulses. And when you unravel them, you will unravel your relationship to all of creation, and see where you recreate the past without being in the present. Once you understand this, you will be able to be in the present, so you can become the fullness of the Seed of Light that you are.

To bend time and space and align to a different frequency, it is important to understand how you have been creating, and how you are currently creating. Ask yourself: *What is my relationship to all that surrounds me?* And see whether you relate to creation and to form from a place of love or fear. For if you relate through fear, and use the energy of fear to create, then your forms will embody fear. Of course, they are truly love at their core, for that is what the source of all creation really is. But it will be love masquerading as fear, for that is what you have asked to come into form. And you will relate to all other forms as fear, not as the pieces of love they truly are. And this is what is happening on a global scale now as the masculine principle begins to die off, as the manifestations of fear and the forms rooted in fear struggle to retain their grip. And instead of allowing the energy of love to come through, those manifestations of fear are trying to maintain the allegiance to form and the privileging of some forms over others. Do not be fooled; it will all pass, eventually. For now, your task is to look closely at the matrix you have inherited.

∞

We are approaching the end of this volume, and we want you to understand a critical point before we reach our final words. The relationship between these matrices, between the impulses around form and energy, are not at all linked inexorably to gender, and so your mother did not necessarily embody the relationship with the energy of the universe, nor did your father with creation, for both were immersed in the collective consciousness. They took on the views of their parents, and so your mother may have expressed a great many views about creation, and your father about the underlying energy of the universe. It is not meant to be a one-to-one correspondence. So focus instead on what traits you absorbed from your parents, without worrying whether the masculine principle aligns with your father, or the feminine principle aligns with your mother. That is not the key. It is instead to understand how your relationships with them structured how you relate to these two impulses (energy and form), for those patterns are the ones that shape the rest of the world. So do not fixate on the alignment between the impulses and your parents' genders.

Once you see how you relate to gender, take that as the place to begin. That is where you must continue to align with the Christ Consciousness through the vehicle of forgiveness, for in forgiving you destroy all separation, and eliminate the past so that your relationships can be in the present. But you can deepen your understanding of the patterns in relationships, and why certain relationships emerge and take certain forms, and other types of relationships are a struggle, or are absent from your life. That is what understanding the matrix—understanding your relationship to all of creation—is about. And as you forgive your parents, those traits and patterns that you have received will begin to lessen. They will soften and dissipate as you remove the separation between you and your parents. Yes, it is possible to live without embodying your parents' karma, and it is through forgiveness that you achieve this liberation from the past, from the parental lineage that dictates how you relate to form, and how you relate to the basic building block of the universe: love.

27. Resilience

You hold the belief that you can simply repair your relationships, and that the patterns you inherited from your parents will then no longer hold sway over you. That is, you will no longer repeat the patterns you learned from your parents, and how you relate to form and energy and time will all somehow be different.

That is not the case, for these patterns are deeply ingrained, and you have reiterated them again and again, so it is not easy to wipe them off. Yes, we have given you the tool of forgiveness, and the various statements that lay claim to who you truly are, and how to be in the moment. But we speak now of your mind's measurements of progress and how much you continue to repeat the same patterns again and again. The mind has the tendency to fall back into old habits—and to berate you for it when you do not act in the liberated manner you think you have achieved. But you must continue to use the tools and dig deeply each and every time your patterns and habits reemerge, not because you cannot leave them in the past, but because the mind does not want you to. The mind is very strong, very capable of turning certain small events into large episodes that warrant very little attention but seem to take a lot of it. So you will need to practice again and again, and in this regard, you are teaching the mind to let go in a way that it does not want to. Because the choices you have made are threatening the ego, which says it will protect you by deploying these patterns, by using the matrix you have absorbed, to fear all the threats that the world poses for you.

We began by transmitting the information we needed to share regarding how you cannot instantly relinquish these matrices that have governed your relationship to form and energy for so long. That is not the way the mind works. You must retrain yourself, through the use of forgiveness, and by becoming aware of the ways in which you relate to these things, and how your parents have shaped your relationships. This is what you do when you privilege form over energy, when you let the physical realm dictate your judgments over and above your knowledge that each person you meet is a Seed of Light, and a divine creation, and that your role is to help them reveal their fullness—even if they don't understand that they are divine or that they have a fullness to share. This is what you have agreed to do in waking up and becoming a part of a much larger movement of people who assist with the planetary ascension and who seek their own growth and enlightenment in the process.

And that is wonderful; we applaud those who are waking up, seeking guidance and direction, and wondering how to proceed. Never fear—the answers will come to you, whether through a close friend, a book, or your own internal guidance. You will know how to proceed. But remember that this path requires perseverance; it requires resilience. You cannot be expected to shed all of your previous understandings and patterns in an instant. And there is nothing wrong with you taking time—yes, taking time—to come to understand the myriad ways in which you have been absorbed by the collective consciousness, and embraced patterns around form and energy from your parents. This is the work of a lifetime. It is the work that you all agreed to do when you came into this realm, at this time.

There is really nothing more important than this, for everything else follows from it. This is not to be grandiose or tell you that you are more important, for this not our point. No, our point is that your willingness to do this kind of work cannot be shirked in favor of something else—in favor of something more trivial, but perhaps more immediately rewarding. The internal labor required to reach a point where you can truly relinquish your attachments to form and identity, and see the perfection in each individual as manifestation of the Divine, is itself an enormous task, and an enormous undertaking.

So understand that your alignment with the Christ Consciousness takes *time*. It will take time in the sense that each of your subsequent co-creations will bring about some change, but your mind will play catch up, and old tendencies will surface. Work through them by forgiving yourself and those involved, and see where that sense of peace and forgiveness takes you.

But do not come with expectations or attachments to how this will look, or how all of your relationships will suddenly become images of or reflections of the Christ, or that you should reject and cut off people who are themselves not trying to follow this path. None of that is the way of the Christ Consciousness, which is to love everything and everybody, all as a manifestation of the Divine. You do not need to reject people in order to maintain your level of purity or uphold your vibration. This is all a form of judgment, making its way through the veiled illusion that you are taking care of yourself, when you are actually artificially closing off parts of your world. No, you must continue to engage and forgive, so you can see how you still carry around the energy of your parents in the way you relate to others, and to all that occurs in your life.

Conclusion

We will end by returning to where we started, with the idea of time and space. We told you that you operate in time and space, and that much of your attention is focused on the past and the future, never the present, and that this relationship with time (and with space) structures your relationships with other people as well. And so your relationships become understandable in and through your construct of time and space. You often assume that the person before you is the person you saw yesterday or two years ago or ten years ago, and that the person will be the same tomorrow. You speak to ghosts and anticipate the same reactions. You never meet them where they are. And this is not a judgment; it is simply a description of your mind as it navigates the co-creation of reality between you and another person when your energies come into contact. You enter each other's fields, and your mind, treating that as an object separate from you, analyzes it according to the information it previously had. This is the mind working to keep you safe and secure in your separation from all others. And so you rely on the memory of past experiences when you see someone, anticipating that the past will also be true in the future.

Those relationships, we said, are often modeled after mothers and fathers, and how your parents raised you and instilled certain patterns in you about the nature of reality. That is, your parents were the entry points into collective consciousness, and this is why you end up resembling them later in life, and why so many of the same patterns appear in families as they are passed down, through teachings and genetics, from one generation to the next, as part of your lineage.

And we spoke of how you relate to fathers and mothers as archetypes, as sources of emotional and material support, and how those archetypes deeply influence your views of certain aspects of reality, namely, the transmutation of energy into form. That is, how the energy that is in everything—the Divine itself, or unconditional love—is transformed into a particular form, with a particular shape, name, and identity. We called this creation.

And we linked these two aspects of reality with the archetypes of the Divine Mother and the Divine Father, and we taught you that this is how you relate to your parents as well—through these associations with archetypes. We talked about how those archetypes are tied to these impulses of energy and creation, and that together this forms the matrix through which you navigate reality, and importantly, all of your relationships.

The key to altering this is to see where those patterns are rooted in fear and separation, and to align with another possibility. This is the teaching of bending time and space, and being able to shape how you relate to time and space, and thereby to shape how your relationships develop. You can speed time up or slow it down, and you can relate to space differently, by how focused you are on the present, in this moment, or how focused you are on another realm, another possibility. We spoke of how your creative faculties are the key to envisioning a new realm. But this is the import of teaching you about the matrix of energy transmuted and transformed into form: Your creative imagination will inevitably draw on the collective consciousness, on the matrix that you already have. You will find yourself recreating the same narratives and dramas, drawn from the belief that you must act and behave in certain ways to ensure your survival, and to feel that you belong in this realm. And so you must be careful that you are not simply aligning to something else, rather than something higher, when you try to bend time and space, when you align with a new possibility. For that possibility may carry forward remnants of what is already there.

There is nothing wrong with that. This is not a cautionary tale in the sense that if you are not careful, you might do something wrong. No—we mean only that your vision of what you think you want, what you think is for your highest good or development, is not always the thing that is actually for your highest good. There is a part of you that must turn it all over to the Divine, to align with a possibility that you cannot fully see or project based on your vision of the past, now extrapolated and projected on the future. There are things you can allow to come to you, and you must be open to possibilities that you cannot imagine, and align to those possibilities without imagining them, without knowing what they are. This is critical if you are trying to help another share their fullness, or allow this person to align to a higher version of him or herself. You cannot determine in advance what that looks like; you cannot simply envision and try to control how their future should be, so that they conform to your model of what the ideal relationship is. That is not a true co-creation in mutuality. That is you trying to control the other person, to mold them to your expectations—even genuine, sincere expectations. And that is the brilliance of what it means to be in a genuine relationship with each other: to stand for the possibility of being in the presence of their fullness, to align with its expression here and now (we mean those words of time and space), so that all may bear witness to that divinity. Yes, that is the nature of genuine relationship, and it means you do not dictate what that fullness looks like, but instead allow it to come into being.

You gave us real formulations so that we could do this with our relationships, and you gave us forgiveness as a technique. But many relationships are just constant co-creations of negativity, of patterns reproducing themselves, so what can we do to undermine those patterns? How do we meet them in a new way?

The question you ask is how to resolve all the difficulties in your relationships, beyond the formulas that we set out earlier, that come from how you relate to each other in time and space. In other words, you have in mind situations where one person simply does not engage or another person constantly uses very negative and perhaps belittling ways of engaging, which leads to all sorts of acrimony and pain. And you are imagining a scenario where you try to speak and confront that other person, asking questions or drawing boundaries and trying to have an honest and open talk about how the other person hurts you. And yet the other person defends or feels threatened, or there is no engagement. And you are wondering how you repair this.

It begins by remembering that not all relationships are going to be repaired in the way you would like, for you imagine the positive outcome to be reconciliation, where the two parties come together in love, and hug and forgive each other. That is not always the case, and in fact, it is *rarely* the case, for it is not always going to be true that both parties strive to align with their highest good or with the highest good of the other so that the other's fullness can find its expression.

For many of you, your relationships will be with those who remain absorbed in the collective consciousness, who continue to adhere to the standard views of separation and who remain threatened by the possibilities of what the world might bring. There will be those who regard all differences in form and identity to be challenges to their own survival and their own claim to belonging in this realm. So your first understanding must be that the co-creation you engage in may not lead to the outcome you expect. And that is where expectation has crept into the relationship. Recall, too, that you believe the outcome must be one of reconciliation and connection; you believe that this is what it means to heal. This is not the case, for healing is your relationship to what is, so that when you are with the other person, no matter what is occurring, you align with their highest good, with their fullness, however that might look. To require an outcome in which you and the other person have resolved all of your differences is an effort to control.

Yes, you can hope this is the outcome and envision it, but recognize this may not be the highest good for all, and that you cannot strive solely to achieve that outcome. You can only attempt to be with this person as the expression of divinity that you are, which means you remain in the present. Do not allow the past to dominate how you interact, or what you say, and do not try to anticipate the future based on their past. You strive always to be with them just as they are, and in holding that space, you may through your presence, through the Seed of Light that you are, shining ever brighter, bring them into alignment with a different version of themselves. This is where you may bend time and space for them, bringing them into a dimension they have not experienced or have only rarely experienced.

That is what you must do, and we have provided tools to

allow that. You may use them and align with their highest good, but remember that this is always an act of co-creation, and the other person has free will and can choose to be in alignment with their ego self as a manifestation of the collective consciousness. This you cannot force; you cannot bully them or persuade them to be otherwise. It will not work, for it will always feel like an imposition. If the person is ready, and if you are meeting them where they are, they may be open to some discussion or spiritual truth and teaching such as this, so that you may help inform them of who they really are. But do not believe your primary means of connection is through the mechanism of the mind, through verbal communication, as a form of information transfer.

You are not going to achieve the types of relationships you want by telling them who they really are or how they should behave. That is not the way. No, you can assist them, gently, to become something more by how you relate to them. In this way, your words will be less focused on how you might persuade them, intellectually, as to their true nature; rather, the energy of your words, as expressions of your true self, will help them get in touch with their true self. The truth is that most people will not be in alignment with their highest selves for much, if any, of their lives. But do not regard this as a failure. This is changing rapidly, as the planet is changing. Every lifetime spent is a precious gift in which each soul moves closer and closer to self-realization. Again, it is not for you to decide how that will happen. You can only stand for the possibility of their fullest expression in the now.

∞

We wish to signal for you where the next volume will take us, and why this work has been so foundational. For we focused in the first volume on the nature of human consciousness and the role of forgiveness and other means of accessing the Christ Consciousness, showing you the true nature of what it means to be human and how you forget this in the face of the collective consciousness. This volume has focused on how you relate to each other, as people, in and through your relationships, and how you use time and space in those relationships. We have endeavored to show you how you can clear your relationships so they are no longer simply products of your lineage, of your past karma, of your views of what the mother and father are as archetypes, and how to relate to time and space in a way that allows you to call forth even greater versions of yourself in the here and the now.

The relationships you have with each other are the building blocks for all of society. Your relationships with yourself, and with your parents, and with others, are the basis for how you navigate all sorts of social concerns. Your organizations move from families to communities to cities to nations and to the globe. In each case, you are relating to larger and larger numbers of individuals, but the relationships are still often the same—built around separation and otherness, so that other becomes a threat to your survival. But this is an old narrative, one that you have played out again and again, and so there is nothing new or original about it.

To put it differently, the forms have changed, but you are still working with an old energy: the energy of fear. The result is that a variety of structures are created to shape and manage your relationships with each other. As you include more and more people in your structures, you create certain lines of power and authority to manage those people. You have laws governing your cities and states and schools and workplaces, and you have economic structures and institutions designed to manage the energy that flows between you, in and through what you call a banking or financial system. You have a political system designed to somehow communicate your collective views about the collective needs, and yet these consistently fall prey to the traps of separation, to traditional views of time and space.

This is the reason that the calling of the Christ Consciousness and the shedding of the collective consciousness is so critical: Because you will continue to replicate newer and newer versions of the same past, all built around separation in time and space, into the future. The forms and names will change, but they will be the same again and again, until all Seeds of Light envision a new reality and align to it. And in the process, you may call in new and different structures to which you can relate. So we will be looking at the law, and politics, and economics, and many other aspects of your system, on a much broader scale, to point to how the role of separation keeps you all in check and affects the planet as a whole. The process of enlightenment and ascension, of the planetary shift as a whole, will not occur in your lifetime, as you are presently experiencing it. It is something that will unfold as many more Seeds of Light come to know who they are.

But it is difficult to live out life in this new way. For many of you, you lose the sense of your divinity as you step outside into the world at large, leaving behind the sacred and safe spaces you have cultivated. For you have begun to create more and more spaces where you can be your highest self, whether through yoga or the spiritual communities that you are forming, or the spread of meditation. All of these are the expansion of the Light in ways that will continue to affect and change how people relate to their own divinity, to their true nature as Seeds of Light.

But the transformation will not occur in an instant. And so we will endeavor to show you how the current structures you have set up are mired in separation, and how you can engage them differently, without falling back into the old habits that have, quite obviously, until now, done only a small amount to actually transform your world. For you inhabit a space of intense imbalance in resources and wealth, intense imbalance in allocation of energy and possibilities, and intense imbalance along lines of identity, where deep wounds prevail and incredible vessels of negative energy remain to be released and transmuted. We will show you how to bring the energy and brilliance of the Christ Consciousness to those institutions in ways that do not necessarily make sense to you now. It is not a question of having everyone in the highest realms of politics or economics or law sit down and meditate. Many people's vision of a world in which everyone sits on a meditation cushion—and we applaud that vision—is a sign of a creative vision of a world that does not currently exist. And yes, there would be a wonderful, joyous world from having everyone meditate, but there is a great deal more transformation that needs to happen.

We speak of the internal transformation that would occur with individual focus on individual consciousness, and that is absolutely fundamental. What we wish to explore in the next book is precisely how those structures would change and shift to accommodate a new consciousness, to look different—not simply what practices need to take place for a new consciousness to emerge. That was the focus of the previous book and this one, and this is work that will be undertaken by all, in time. But what would the world look like if it were based on a consciousness that does not start from separation, but from the awareness that everything that is experienced is the purest expression of love? That the energy of the universe is pure love, and the creation that can come with the awareness of that truth is vastly different from what you have presently created? With our next book, we will impart a vision of what that world can look like.

As we come to a close, we want to express our immeasurable love to all of you. You are so deeply loved by us, by the Divine, by the Universe as a whole, which is the physical expression of God itself. Understand that it is all made of love, and so are you. You are love, you are loved, and you are in the process of ascending to a higher state. Know this to be true, hold it in your hearts, and watch as the world shifts around you. That is your gift, your power—to bend time and space—and in so doing, to call in a new realm, a new consciousness: the Christ Consciousness that is now available to you all.

Coda

This is a brief coda to this volume, which will seal its energetic signature and allow it to be sent forth into the world. Much has transpired since this volume's original transmittal, and we wish to add a final update to its contents.

We wish to provide you with a new way of being in this world, a new way of being in relationship with others, and to relate to them without the emotional weight of the past. And to do this, we have shown how you can bend time, by being with it, without judgment, without any kind of requirement that the present moment be different from what it is. And what is transpiring now is that you each have a choice, the choice of free will—to choose to be in alignment with what is, as you perceive it, or to align with a higher vision of what is, and to therefore be with the present not as you perceive it, but as it really is. The present already exists as that higher vision, but you are not experiencing time and space in this way. No, you are experiencing time and space through the limitations of your current consciousness, which is filled with judgment and the requirement that the world be different. But you do not know how to make the world different; you do not know yet how to change it.

For now, the important step is how you relate to this world, as it currently appears to you. You perceive it to be flawed, filled with misery and corruption, and it is as you have constructed it. But it is also, equally, a world of magic and wonder, that exists simultaneously, at the same moment as what you have constructed. Imagine that the world is made of Light and you have simply made it resemble darkness, as if molding the Light into darkness. It is still Light, is made up of Light, even as it resembles and looks like darkness. That is what you have created.

But you can relate to it as Light, and allow it to shine more brightly. To do so, we offer the following mantra or affirmation—a statement or claim to truth—that you can use to constitute yourself in this very moment: *I am the Christ in form reborn. I am the Light in form reborn.* That is what you truly are. And so you can claim your divinity at any moment, in any experience or situation, and reaffirm your perception that what is before you is the illusion generated, co-created, by your fellow human beings, as they perceive the world through the muddy lens of the collective consciousness. It is your ability to stay present to what truly is—Light masquerading as darkness—that allows you to recall the truth, the fundamental truth, that all that surrounds you is pure love. That is all reality is, and all that you are, too. Recall that in each moment, at every moment, and the world will bend around you to become Light again.

That is the way to change the world. Change your relationship to it, and the world will become Light again.

Acknowledgments

Every book is a unique creation. The process is never quite the same, from one book to the next. Although this book was channeled, it was not the first-born child, so to speak, and therefore had to contend with arriving into the world with an older sibling. The manuscript was downloaded starting in May 2016, but it had to wait until the first child, *Seeds of Light*, was published and given time to grow. So the manuscript sat patiently, waiting for its debut. When the time came to prepare it for publication, I had learned that readers needed more assistance with the dense ideas contained in these transmissions, and so I worked more carefully to pare it down and make it as accessible as possible. As a result, *Bending Time* underwent far more revision than its predecessor. On this score, I cannot thank my copy editor, Carrie White, enough for her careful edits, judicious suggestions, and supreme patience. Without her input, *Bending Time* would be far less legible. I also owe a special debt of gratitude to Cynthia Lamb, a fellow channel who read an early draft of this work and gave me immensely helpful feedback. Many thanks to you both for helping to bring this work into the world.

I remain in awe of this entire process, without a full understanding of why I have been given this role, and what it means for my life. I simply trust this experience of being transmitted these teachings, and remain open to being led. It is not always an easy path to be a living channel for disembodied wisdom; in many ways, a so-called conventional life as a lawyer is less challenging, at least when it comes to explaining your life's work at a dinner party. But I have come to accept that living a conventional life was never my path. As the celebrated channel and empath Paul Selig (to whom I owe a debt of gratitude for his guidance), once said to me, "The path has chosen you." I am beyond grateful for this path, wherever it leads, and for the Light Beings who speak through me. I am deeply humbled by the service they have selected me to perform.

I have had numerous teachers and guides, all of whom

have contributed, in ways large and small, to my own personal transformation: Amma, Mother Meera, Karunamayi, William McGreal, Tony LeRoy, Paul Selig, and William Linville. My supreme gratitude goes to my primary teacher, Mirabai Devi, who has lovingly guided me to this path over many years, and to Will McGreal, with whom I can lose track of time talking about time and consciousness. Thank you both for helping me to see my potential and become who I am today.

I am also deeply blessed to have a number of cherished friends and family members without whom my life would be considerably impoverished: Alisha A., Rex E., Jay D., Dara G., Rebecca G., Anu G., Laura J., Drew J., Erin L., Alan F., Gil F., Kate F., Stu F., Diane. F., Patricia H., Katie L., Sally N., Jeff R., Dana R., Andrew S., George T., Drew T., Mara V., and Lindsey W. Thank you for love and support over the years.

My most heart-felt thanks go to my beloved husband, Max, whose unconditional love and unwavering support for my work are precious gifts, and to Lily and Charlie, whose feline shenanigans bring me so much joy and comedic relief. Each moment with you is a miracle.

About the Author

Patrick Paul Garlinger experienced a dramatic spiritual awakening years ago when he began to meet numerous spiritual teachers and experience higher states of consciousness. While completing his training under the renowned spiritual teacher, Mirabai Devi, Patrick underwent an awakening of his kundalini and began to channel works of spiritual wisdom. *Bending Time* is the second of three volumes of writing transmitted to him between March and September 2016. *Seeds of Light: Channeled Transmissions on the Christ Consciousness*, published in March 2017, was the first volume. In 2016, he published *When Thought Turns to Light: A Practical Guide to Spiritual Transformation*, a highly accessible introduction to spiritual techniques for readers seeking to incorporate more peace, joy, and wonder into their everyday lives, which won the 2017 Living Now Spirit Book Award.

Patrick lives in New York City, where he provides spiritual guidance and healing services. For more information about his books and services, please visit: www.patrickpaulgarlinger.com.

CPSIA information can be obtained
at www.ICGtesting.com
Printed in the USA
LVHW09s0317280918
591646LV00001B/2/P